Fishing on Wednesday
Finding Freedom Through Entrepreneurship

BEN T. ALEXANDER

Copyright © 2018 Benjamin T. Alexander

All rights reserved.

ISBN: 1985606062
ISBN-13: 978-1985606067

To my daughters, Claire and Grace

TABLE OF CONTENTS

1	The Crazy Englishman	1
2	Money River	3
3	Kongō Gumi	7
4	The Late Bloomer	9
5	Pink Cadillacs	12
6	Profits from Dirt	15
7	Boomerangs in Tampa	19
8	Mary Jane, Tilapia and Catamarans	22
9	Lord of the Flies	26
10	The $66 Million Woman	28
11	An Elephant and 15 Criminals	30
12	Drawing Cats	35
13	Fishing on Wednesday	37
14	Dark Motives	40
15	Your Trillion-Dollar Business	42
16	Booms and Busts	45
17	You Can Write Your Story	48
18	Why Now?	49
19	Marcus Lemonis	50
20	Your Most Valuable Asset	52
21	The Importance of Mentors	54

22	Systems Matter	56
23	Start with Sales	59
24	Traditional Businesses	63
25	Patents and Licensing	65
26	Buying a Franchise	68
27	Real Estate	70
28	Strategic Partnerships	72
29	Direct Sales	74
30	Know Your Numbers	77
31	Cold Water	79

THE ENGLISHMAN

When dealing with entrepreneurs always expect the unexpected. That being said, I never anticipated going to a homebuilt shooting range on New Year's Eve to usher in 2015, by why the hell not? There I was, sipping booze and shooting AR-15 semiautomatics on a mild South Florida night with one of the wildest guys I know: Marcus Price.

To be entirely fair to Marcus, his unconventional path has made him enormously wealthy, so I can't possibly fault him for it. Marcus had posted on social media that he was holding his annual Guns and Beer New Year's Eve Blowout Party at his spread out in the boonies. Despite having known Marcus for years, I'd never been to his house, so I bought a case of Coors and hit the road early.

Marcus lives on 20 acres of Florida real estate complete with a sprawling main house and a guest house bigger than most average homes. In the main house, Marcus and his wife, M.J., decorated eight huge Christmas trees with enough string lights to illuminate a stadium. It was over-the-top and fun, just like Marcus and MJ, but the ornate decorations inside the mansion paled in comparison to Marcus's backyard.

Before the rest of the guests arrived, Marcus spent a few minutes showing me all the stuff he had on his land. Using a backhoe and some heavy equipment, Marcus had erected a firing range behind his home complete with a safety backstop made from telephone poles. On a folding table near the range was an assortment of ammunition, semi-automatic machine guns, handguns and hearing protection.

Finally, Marcus took me to see his twins: two full-sized bucket trucks identical to the models the local electric company uses. At this point, my curiosity got the best of me.

"Marcus, why on earth do you own two bucket trucks?"

Marcus smiled. "Because two are better than one!"

It was difficult in that moment to imagine Marcus's humble

beginnings, but I knew his story all too well. Marcus Price came to the United States as a broke hitchhiker in the 1990s and tried anything and everything to make a buck. Today, Marcus is the CEO of Goin' Postal, a chain of 250 mailbox stores that he and M.J. started over a decade ago. Marcus has always been a big thinker; he's not afraid to be outrageous, take risks and live life on his own terms. He took a pragmatic concept and created a business with unlimited potential. With the right partnerships, Goin' Postal could open thousands of new stores over the next few decades, but Marcus's story of success is far from atypical in the world of entrepreneurship.

Business ownership has always been the fastest (and most lawful) way to go from rags to riches in a few years. If an entrepreneur lives in a free country and comes up with a concept that meets a significant demand, there is potentially no limit to what that person can create.

I encourage entrepreneurship not only for the income, but also for the freedom. Entrepreneurship means having the flexibility to do anything at any time with the people who matter most. For Marcus, it means having two bucket trucks just because he can. For me, it means living a debt-free life with my family. While there is initially a degree of unpredictability to the entrepreneurial lifestyle, a true entrepreneur ultimately exercises a large amount of control over his or her destiny. If someone launches the right concept at the right time, there is limitless possibility.

Entrepreneurship is simply defined as going forth, and this is a fitting definition. Every job, manufactured object and business requires someone to go forth and take action for the success of the venture. There is ample opportunity for anyone to join the world-changing expedition of business ownership. Therefore, through this book, I hope to encourage more people to join their fellow entrepreneurs on the great unexpected journey of trade and commerce.

MONEY RIVER

In order to understand entrepreneurship, it is helpful to think of the larger economy like a river. When someone launches a business, it's as if that person is bravely pushing a boat into the river. If the business is successful, the entrepreneur's boat will float along the stream of prosperity. If the business isn't profitable, the boat will sink.

Now, let's say an entrepreneur's boat proves unseaworthy. That person will be left with two choices: either give up and drown or persevere and swim. In the latter situation, a stalwart entrepreneur can regroup on the shore and launch another vessel. It is important to remember that no matter how many boats sink (and no matter the circumstances of sinking), there can always be another boat.

Some entrepreneurs keep it simple with small boats, handing their modest but navigable vessels down to their children and grandchildren. Others brace the currents in tiny rafts and, after many years of hard work, see those rafts grow into billion-dollar supertankers.

Of course, a person can always work as a crewmember on other people's boats. Good boats need good helmsmen, boatswains and quartermasters. These people can sometimes call the shots, boss around the apprentices and even steer the ship, but no matter what they do, they will almost never own the boats on which they work. Their fate will always be at the mercy of their captains who could kick them into the river on a whim.

For those who want to be better, more reliable deckhands, the study of entrepreneurship (and, by extension, this book) is moot. This book is for the unruly and unconventional minds, the Marcus Prices of the world who want the boat, mansion, twin bucket trucks and all the additional perks that come with successful business ownership. Everyone else can earn an MBA and learn how to better swab the deck.

That being said, a boat's survival depends on more than steadfast deckhands and capable captains. There are many variables, such as the engineering of the boat, how it is steered, the method of propulsion and even the nature of the cargo.

Another large factor is the river itself. Some rivers have reliable currents that can carry boats for many miles. Others might have dangerous rapids ready to send a crew splashing into the water. Even worse, droughts can sabotage the paths of even the most seaworthy vessels, leaving everyone's boats abandoned on the riverbed. Because of this, it's important to know which river a business is in and to plan accordingly.

When observing the history of the global economy, it's easy to see when society experienced high and low tides in the worldwide economic waters. Giant rivers that carried many ships to prosperity sometimes turned to waterfalls, smashing every boat in spectacular fashion.

During the height of the Roman Empire, businesses flourished in the territories surrounding the Mediterranean. The Romans had the largest economy in the world complete with fixed currency, an organized military and advanced mining operations across Europe. Historians estimate that, at the time, the Roman Empire accounted for nearly a quarter of the global GDP. For many years, Rome's economic river was the most profitable in the world.

Eventually, Rome succumbed to invasions, and the economic torch went to China. Entrepreneurs thrived under the Song Dynasty, and trade prospered with India and East Africa. Nearly any Chinese entrepreneur who launched a profitable business during the Song Dynasty experienced wild success; the current was strong and the timing ideal.

After the Mongols invaded China, disease, instability and provincial battles ruined China's industrial health. This allowed the Mughal Empire's economic river to expand, giving India the chance to flaunt its pecuniary prowess. After a long economic boom, however, the cycle continued; the Mughal Empire fell to the British Empire. The Industrial Revolution paired with the economic output of the British colonies allowed British businesses to dominate the world stage for decades.

In this scenario, the Crown eventually undermined its own interests. The British Empire built its economic might on the subjugation of the colonies. It was only a matter of time before the colonies began to yearn for freedom. By the early 1900s, many countries had declared independence from colonial rule and doomed the British economic river.

The largest economy that emerged in the 20th century came from a relatively new nation. It was a constitutional republic with tremendous amounts of raw resources such as iron, coal and arable farmland. The Atlantic and Pacific oceans granted this nation geographic protection and allowed courageous immigrants of all ethnic backgrounds to try their hands at economic fortune. The American dream birthed itself as the British Empire diminished. To this day, American capitalism continues to dominate the global economic current.

Though this dynamic global economic history may alarm a burgeoning entrepreneur seeking stability, it's important to once again consider the plight of those who will never own ships. These people control neither the flow of the river nor the vessels on which they ride. Entrepreneurs, on the other hand, have mastery over one of these variables: the ship. While no river is safe forever, owning the ship gives entrepreneurs command over their lives in ways that typical employment doesn't.

Consider one of the largest supertankers on the river, Walmart. Sam Walton launched Walmart in 1962 with a single humble store in Rogers, Arkansas. He set a little boat afloat in a trickling economic stream worlds away from the rapids many entrepreneurs enjoy today. Sam Walton took control of his destiny by owning the boat, and that once-tiny vessel is now one of the largest companies on the planet. In 2016, Walmart sold $482 billion worth of underwear, kitty litter, spoons and any other knickknack you could possibly want. That's $1.3 billion per day, $54 million per hour, $900,000 per minute and $15,000 per second.

In the next 30 years, captains and deckhands alike will experience tumultuous waters as technology alters the landscape of the global economy. Unfathomable inventions will create trillions of dollars in opportunity.

According to futurist and best-selling author Ray Kurzweil, technology will advance exponentially between the years 2020 and 2050. Astounding developments in robotics, artificial intelligence and renewable energy will change the course of the economic river. By 2040, some of the concepts that are tiny start-ups today will grow to be global beasts that generate billions of dollars in revenue per day.

In 2015, American businesses generated $18 trillion, or 22 percent of the total global economic output, despite only comprising five percent of the world's population. America's nearest competitor is China, and several projections show the USA and China both hitting the $22 trillion (GDP) mark by 2025.

For entrepreneurs, especially American entrepreneurs, this is the right place and the right time. The river is wide, fast and deep with enough room for millions of boats. There is no lack of water, strong currents or opportunity. Most importantly, there are no excuses.

KONGŌ GUMI

In 593 A.D., three carpenters finished construction on the first Buddhist temple in Japan, Shitennō-ji. As with most accomplishments lucky enough to be called 'first', the construction of this temple came with an added degree of uncertainty. While key members of the Japanese royal family practiced Buddhism and had even commissioned the temple's creation, the majority of Japanese people were unaccustomed to the practices of this foreign religion.

During the building process, one of these carpenters decided to start his own temple construction business, a bold move in a country unfamiliar with Buddhism. His name was Shigemitsu Kongō, and while modern people could hardly know what was going through his mind when he founded Kongō Gumi back in 578 A.D., people have to wonder what he would say if he could see his business today.

That's right, today.

Shitennō-ji still stands and is a popular travel destination for both tourists and religious pilgrims alike. Like most major religious sites, it has stood for hundreds of years to bear testament to new generations seeking a connection with the divine. What makes Shitennō-ji especially remarkable, however, is that its many renovations have been carried out not only by the same company, but by the same family.

In the last 1,400 years, the wooden temple has suffered fires, floods and all forms of natural calamities. Despite this, Kongō Gumi has rebuilt the temple time and time again, always reflecting the style of its original construction. Kongō Gumi carried out its last major renovation of Shitennō-ji in 1963.

For 40 generations, Kongō Gumi prevailed as a profitable family business through over a thousand years of dynastic cycles, wars and various disasters. To put this in perspective, consider that the business launched only one generation after the fall of the Roman Empire. When Guttenberg invented the printing press, Kongō Gumi was already a thousand years old. The company was already 1200 years old when George Washington was inaugurated!

The Kongō family was so renowned that most men who married into the family gladly took the Kongō surname as a sign of respect. Kongō Gumi even has a meters-long scroll recording the name of every son or daughter who took over the corporation.

While Kongō Gumi's work has always centered around the construction of temples, the business ensured its longevity by adapting to the times. When temple work waned during WWII, Kongō Gumi began to manufacture ornate wooden coffins to make up for the loss in revenue. Even today, the company does about 20 percent of its business outside of the realm of temple building, though its main source of income is still the same after many centuries of development.

Despite the fact that Takamastu Construction Group now owns Kongō Gumi, the descendants of Shigemitsu Kongō still work for the company to this day.

Shigemitsu Kongō created the world's oldest independent company from a simple idea that fed and clothed his family for 14 centuries, and the company still creates boatloads of revenue to this day. Could you start a small enterprise right now that benefits your progeny for decades to come?

THE LATE BLOOMER

No one would look at the early life of Harland Sanders and peg him for greatness. Sanders was born to a typical farming family in rural Indiana during the summer of 1890, but his father died only five years later, leaving his mother destitute. While Sanders's mother struggled to support the family with her job at a tomato cannery, Sanders spent his days foraging for food to feed himself and his younger siblings. Sanders's mother eventually remarried, but Sanders and his brother often butted heads with their new stepfather, an abusive alcoholic who would beat his stepsons at the slightest provocation.

Sanders dropped out of school in seventh grade and eventually falsified papers to enter the armed forces at age 15. He later worked as a blacksmith's assistant at a railroad company through his uncle's connections, but he lost his job after getting into a fistfight with a coworker.

While working for the railroad company, Sanders had completed a mail-order law school correspondence course and passed the bar exam in Arkansas. What started as a promising legal career ended in shambles only three years later, however, when Sanders got into a courtroom brawl with his own client.

For the next few years, Sanders tried his hand at several trades and eventually found himself in the fuel business. He ran a gas station for Standard Oil, but the Great Depression hit, and Sanders found himself out of work again. In 1930, Shell Oil offered him ownership of a run-down gas station and restaurant in Corbin, Kentucky. It was at this restaurant that Sanders perfected his fried chicken recipe involving a pressure cooker and eleven herbs and spices.

In the mid-1930s, Sanders expanded the Corbin restaurant by adding a hotel only to see that hotel and restaurant burn down in 1939. Sanders rebuilt his business, but gas rationing during WWII stemmed the flow of patrons to the restaurant. He managed to keep the restaurant in

Corbin, but he had to work another job to pay his bills. At this point, Sanders was 51 years old.

For the next decade, Sanders bounced around from job to job. It wasn't until 1952 that he sold his fried chicken recipe to a restaurant in Salt Lake City for a percentage of the sales. Within a year, the Salt Lake City restaurant had tripled its sales on the strength of Sanders's juicy and delicious chicken.

Back in Kentucky, the government built a new interstate. It cut off virtually all the customer traffic to Sanders's restaurant in Corbin, which forced him into a difficult yet unavoidable decision. Sanders sold the restaurant at auction, with all proceeds going towards debt he owed on the building.

Sanders found himself at 65 years old with practically nothing. He received $105 per month from social security. He was flat broke with nothing to show for a lifetime of hard work except a fried chicken recipe in his pocket. He regularly received a small commission from the Salt Lake City location, so he hit the road and tried to sell his chicken recipe to more restaurants.

For the next two years, Sanders slept in the back of his car. He would drive thousands of miles to cook fried chicken for potential prospects, thus establishing the humble beginnings of the Kentucky Fried Chicken chain.

When Sanders was 74, he sold KFC for $2 million while remaining with the company as a spokesperson. When he died at the ripe old age of 90, KFC was a fast food powerhouse with 6,000 locations and over $2 billion in annual revenue.

As of 2016, KFC has 20,000 stores worldwide.

Sanders was far from a perfect person with a perfect business model. He had personal flaws and a volatile temper, but his story of many losses followed by rampant success is an inspiration to anyone who has ever failed. He lost jobs, got into fights, went broke and watched his livelihood literally burn. Despite this, he had the fortitude and grit to go out and build a new business every single time.

Most people who find themselves broke at 65 would simply give up and fade away into the anonymity of poverty. Sanders was made from tougher stuff; he was stubborn, persistent and confident. He knew his fried chicken recipe was amazing and never gave up on his idea.

The creativity and persistence Sanders demonstrated in his lifetime of failures would have made him successful in any era. He kept trying to be a prosperous entrepreneur even when it was probably easier to keep a low-hanging job and lead an unremarkable life. Grit and determination will always be a huge part of any meaningful success.

If an entrepreneur launches a little business onto the economic river, that boat might capsize; it is an inevitable risk. Sanders sunk a bunch of ships before his chicken recipe kept him above water. Keep Sanders in mind when the going gets tough; he kept at it, and now he's a legend.

PINK CADILLACS

It was the summer of 1977. Ginger Buchanon was a runaway in her early teens living on the streets of Dallas, Texas. At 11 years old she had run away from a broken and dysfunctional home. To make money, she would take odd jobs and panhandle when no one was hiring.

On this particular day, Ginger was begging for change in front of a hair salon when a professional, well-dressed woman with a pink Cadillac approached her and asked if she had eaten that day. Ginger hadn't, so when the woman offered to take her home and give her a meal, Ginger eagerly accepted the invitation.

The woman took Ginger home, fed her, let her wash herself and gave her a clean set of clothes. The woman then told Ginger that she could stay in the house for a few days, but the extravagant display of charity embarrassed Ginger, so Ginger left by the end of the day.

Before the two parted ways, the woman in the pink Cadillac gave Ginger her business card and asked her to call anytime. This, Ginger decided, was an act of altruism she could accept.

Fifteen years passed. Ginger got off the streets, and when she moved into a new apartment, she found the business card. It was pink and printed on high-quality paper: "Mary Kay Ash, Founder and President, Mary Kay Cosmetics."

Ginger Buchanon is a friend and business associate of mine in Tampa. When I told her I was writing about the founder of Mary Kay Cosmetics, she shared this story with me.

Mary Kay Ash, like Harland Sanders, came from fairly unremarkable beginnings. She grew up in a sleepy Texas town, got married young and had three children. After her husband returned from serving in WWII, the two divorced. Ash, determined to support herself on her own terms, obtained a job in direct sales.

When Ash was 45 years old, her employer passed her up on a promotion and gave it to a man she had trained. At this point, she quit her sales job and decided to write a book about women in business. As she began writing, she realized that she had inadvertently drafted a business plan for what could be a great company.

Initially, Ash had planned to start this business with her new husband, but when he suddenly died of a heart attack a mere month after the couple wed, Ash's plans were put on hold. Finally, in 1971, Ash took a $5,000 investment and started Mary Kay Cosmetics with her 20-year-old son, Richard Rogers.

Ash was a woman of faith who built her business on the Golden Rule. She crafted a direct sales business model that allowed any woman to start a business for $100 and develop income by creating a sales network. Ash's company took multi-level marketing to the next level and went international in the 1980s, earning worldwide respect.

Since 1971, thousands of Mary Kay business owners have built a steady income through a network of customers, many earning hundreds of thousands of dollars a year as a result.

Mary Kay Cosmetics rewards top business builders by granting them a 24-month lease on a pink Cadillac. If business owners keep their sales numbers at a certain threshold, the company pays the monthly payments on their leases. A pink Cadillac on the road almost always has a successful Mary Kay Cosmetics business owner at the wheel.

When Ash passed away in 2001, she had over a hundred business awards to her name including the Horatio Alger Award and a spot in the Business Hall of Fame. Fortune magazine lauded Mary Kay Cosmetics as one of the best companies in the USA for its salespeople. Ash accomplished this not only by paying her business owners fairly, but also by taking an interest in them on a personal level.

There are many accounts of Ash's benevolence from people like Ginger Buchanon; Ash did everything from visiting some of her salespeople in the hospital to sending notes on people's birthdays. She called her business owners her daughters. Seeing that recognition was just as important for morale as a paycheck, Ash created a reward system for good and consistent salesmanship. She even established charitable foundations to help women who suffered from domestic violence and funded women's cancer research. Ash understood the human element of business, and this is part of what made her so wildly successful.

Mary Kay Cosmetics is now an international powerhouse with annual sales of $3.5 billion and over 3 million global distributors. The long-term success of Mary Kay Cosmetics came from the founder's integrity and character as well as the direct sales aspect of her business model.

Ash's business gave millions of people a chance to get into entrepreneurship for a nominal fee. The Mary Kay Cosmetics corporate team built the systems needed to train people in sales, manufacture products and support the worldwide distributor network.

In the end, Ash made a positive difference in the lives of countless individuals, including people like Ginger Buchanon who never even joined the business. Ash saw a need in the marketplace for a business that could empower women, and when she saw that no one else was meeting that need, she went forth and created her business.

Mary Kay Cosmetics is a company built on fundamental values. This is one of the reasons it has longevity and relevance in the marketplace. Mary Kay Ash wanted to help women first; profitability was a secondary concern. She helped everyone from the most successful salespeople in her company to a young runaway named Ginger; who knows how many other people she helped in her lifetime.

PROFITS FROM DIRT

Jonathan Brewer was 8 years old when he went to the White House for the annual Easter Egg Roll. His father worked at the Pentagon, and many families of higher-level government officials attended this event. Then-President John F. Kennedy was strolling about the lawn, tossing footballs and chatting with the children, when a Secret Service agent approached and whispered something in Kennedy's ear. At that moment, Kennedy gently handed the ball to Brewer and left the event.

The date was April 8th, 1963, a tragic day in United States naval history. The nuclear submarine *USS Thresher* had gone missing some 220 miles east of Boston. Later, the government would learn that the submarine experienced catastrophic equipment failure and sunk, claiming the lives of 129 men in the cold waters of the North Atlantic. The event affected millions of people living in the US, including young Jonathan Brewer. For Brewer, however, this wouldn't be the only time he found himself at the crossroads of history.

During his early 20s, Brewer labored in various positions at Amtrak and quickly worked his way from a redcap role carrying bags for passengers to a cushy corporate position. After that, he went from a junior management job at Amtrak's national headquarters to a corner office with a generous salary in material management.

One day, he was looking out the window of his Philadelphia office when the big question hit.

"Is this it?" Brewer asked himself. "If I died today, would anybody know I existed? Am I making a difference?"

Brewer realized then and there that he didn't like the answer to that nagging question. He quit his safe and lucrative job with Amtrak, bought a Jeep and moved to Nevada to become a gold prospector. For years, Brewer mined enough gold on his claims to pay his bills while also becoming an expert in mining and heavy-duty processing equipment. This led him to a short stint in residential and commercial real estate sales while attending Sierra College to earn certification in pyro and hydrometallurgy.

Brewer gained a decent reputation as a process engineer, and two South Korean investors in Sacramento eventually recruited him to evaluate a soil processing plant and a handful of patents. The investors had purchased two small American companies that specialized in eliminating environmental contaminants from soil and were preparing to finalize patents on new oxidative soil washing technology.

The economic boom between 1960 and 1990 had created tons of industrial soil contamination all over South Korea, establishing a need for new technology to mitigate this problem. The investors made the broad assumption that an easy solution for the dilemma could be purchased in America and shipped back home. As with most 'easy solutions', this plan proved to be far more difficult to implement that the investors had initially assumed.

By the 1990s, soil contamination was a huge global issue. The *Exxon Valdez* had run aground in Prince William Sound, and large companies that had polluted sites in the recent past encountered huge legal battles due to the ever-growing problem. Hauling away polluted sand and soil was expensive. Dumping the soil in hazardous waste landfills still created long-term liability for the companies that caused the initial problems. Brewer began to understand the soil remediation industry as he helped the investors develop their portable processing equipment. This equipment cleaned contaminated soil on the spot, which was a far more cost-effective option than hauling it somewhere else.

While Brewer was able to conform existing South Korean equipment into a reliable system, the processing cost and lack of production throughput doomed the system's potential in the US market. Brewer recognized that using landfills was not sustainable in the long haul, but this seemingly 'cheap' South Korean alternative would be difficult to sell to American consumers.

The investors eventually shut down their American operations and returned to South Korea to implement the conformed technology. They asked Brewer to join them, but he politely declined, as he was not a person who fully appreciated the finer points of kimchi.

At this point, Brewer was 40 years old and, by choice, unemployed. Despite this, he had direction. With savings in the bank, lots of soil processing experience and a solid foundation in inorganic chemistry, he believed he was the guy who could develop a winning invention in the soil remediation niche. This could open up huge economic opportunities in that sector.

Brewer sat down with large easel sheets of paper and made a list of 20 parameters that his equipment would have to meet in order to succeed in the global market. He recognized right away that there were gaps in his knowledge of technical subjects like organic chemistry, so he enrolled in a handful of courses at his local community college.

While Brewer began to develop the chemical and organic processes necessary for his concept, he also worked on the equipment side of his idea. The design would be a portable unit that processed soil on-site at a fraction of what it would cost to haul it elsewhere. This design was so different from the current environmental technology; Brewer feared that his idea was too ambitious, but nevertheless, he persisted.

Brewer purchased a wire-feed MIG welder at a construction supply warehouse and learned how to use it via old VHS tapes, employing the time-tested trial-and-error method. His knowledge of metallurgy and mineral science from his railroad and mining years came in handy as he began experimenting in his garage.

Eventually, Brewer launched a Sacramento-based company called EarthWorks Environmental and built his first soil-cleaning unit for less than $10,000. It was a self-contained machine that people could tow behind a pickup truck and take anywhere. Brewer initially used his savings to build the first unit. Today, EarthWorks is a viable, self-sustaining company that fuels its own growth with income alone.

In the early '90s, there were plenty of tech startups in California; these small companies would often garner millions of dollars in funding before earning a single penny of revenue. Brewer watched friends, entrepreneurs and professional associates start these new ventures, burn through other people's money and then fizzle out a year or two later.

Brewer chose a different path. He took his one and only prototype on the road and landed small soil remediation contracts at secure sites across the country. He proved his concept and its ability to make money. Over the next two years, he generated $300,000 in gross revenue with admirable margins. This money went back into the business to fund his patent. Brewer ran his operation lean while learning about the marketplace and the potential demand for his service and process.

As Brewer watched other companies crash and burn during the economic bubble of 1999, he successfully moved through the patent process with the technology he had developed. Soil remediation wasn't sexy; it never will be. Cleaning fuel, oil and chemical contaminants isn't a glamorous job, but Brewer made sure his equipment did the job better than anything else on the market. Brewer knew there would be a growing global demand for EarthWorks's technology; he just had to learn how to tap into that market. Besides, while the work is far from elegant, it's perhaps one of the most crucial jobs on the planet. Environmental issues affect everyone.

People began to recognize the genius in what Brewer was doing. His technology attracted the attention of the engineering department at the University of California. It won the award for "Most Innovative New Product" in the Transportation and Environment category in 2001.

In 2002, EarthWorks completed its patent process and began marketing and selling soil remediation equipment around the globe using only the Internet. Brewer has remained largely debt-free despite the many hurdles he encountered and is now learning new lessons as he introduces his equipment to five continents.

If Brewer had stayed at Amtrak, he would have made a decent income, but his story would be far less interesting. He never would have learned about gold mining, MIG welding, organic chemistry or entrepreneurship. EarthWorks would never have existed.

Inside a shop in Safety Harbor, Florida, Brewer still spends countless hours developing new uses for his machines. He has a full life; he spends plenty of time volunteering with Rotary, seeing his grandchildren and going to church. He continues to develop an amazing business that betters the planet.

EarthWorks may never be a billion-dollar giant. Brewer isn't interested in that kind of life, but the revenue from this business has given Brewer a sense of purpose that he never would have found working in corporate America. Brewer made a difference in the future of the planet and, by extension, humanity. If that isn't being in the right place at the right time at the crossroads of history, I don't know what is.

When Brewer asks himself if he's making a difference in the world today, the answer is clear.

BOOMERANGS IN TAMPA

Every great business starts with a big idea, but no one can ever truly control when that big idea is going to strike. For Bob Basham and Chris Sullivan, it came to them at a jazz club in Tampa.

"We wrote the word 'Outback' in red lipstick on a mirror." Sullivan wrote in an interview.

"One of my co-founders, Bob Basham, along with our wives and myself were in a jazz club talking about a new restaurant idea and what to call it. Lacking pen and paper, Bob's wife reached into her purse. In an innovative maneuver that foreshadowed many to come in the business we were creating, she then turned to the mirror. One hour and one tube of lipstick later, the Outback Steakhouse brand was born.

"It was 1987. Crocodile Dundee was a recent Hollywood splash, Australia's Bicentennial was getting lots of press in the United States and the America's Cup was taking place Down Under. [America's] fascination with Australia had made it the number-one desired destination for travelers here in Tampa, Florida. We guessed that was true in other parts of the US as well.

"Tampa had a void in the casual steakhouse market. The casual steakhouses that did exist here and around the country were nearly all Western-themed restaurants whose brands were undifferentiated. We saw an Australian concept as different but consistent with people's expectations for a casual steakhouse. 'Outback' had a casual, come-as-you-want feel, and 'Outback Steakhouse' was both easily spoken and easily remembered."

In 1988, Chris Sullivan, Bob Basham, Tim Gannon and Trudy Cooper started the first Outback Steakhouse on Henderson Road in Tampa. None of the partners had ever been to Australia. Basham and Sullivan had both worked for Brinker International, the conglomerate behind Chili's, so they knew how to scale one location into a national brand. Outback Steakhouse focused on fresh ingredients and made-from-scratch recipes;

the concept took off almost immediately.

The Outback Steakhouse chain was the beginning of OSI Restaurant Partners, which would go on to launch brands such as Carrabba's Italian Grill, Fleming's Prime Steakhouse & Wine Bar and Bonefish Grill. In 2006, Bain Capital bought OSI for $3 billion and changed the name to Bloomin' Brands.

Today, Bob Basham is 70 years old. When I met him, he was handing out food to customers at a new restaurant concept called PDQ. He humbly introduced himself only as "Bob," and it wasn't until I'd met him a few times that I went home and read about all the things he had accomplished.

Basham is a calm, humble man who doesn't seek the limelight. Basham would show up at PDQ grand openings to simply serve his team and mingle with customers. He started the PDQ chain in 2011; by the end of 2016, PDQ had opened 55 restaurants across the country.

Basham built a strong team at PDQ, and his investors know that he has 45 years of proven restaurant, operations and marketing experience. If you walk into a PDQ today, you will notice the inviting and sunny design of the space, excellent food and original concept.

When I saw Basham recently, I asked him a question: "You've already reached the brass ring of success with Outback and OSI. Why start a new chain at this season in your life?"

Basham gave it some thought and replied, "The restaurant business gets in your blood and stays in your blood. It's fun and challenging to grow an idea and work with all these great young people. I can only golf so much; I love being around the energy of our team."

One of the keys to Basham's wealth is the opportunity he created (and continues to create) for hundreds of thousands of people. PDQ has formed 3,800 jobs, and Bloomin' Brands has generated $4.4 billion in sales with over 100,000 current employees. That isn't counting all of the people who have previously worked for Basham's ventures since 1988, not to mention the peripheral effect of employment on all the communities where an Outback Steakhouse or PDQ is located. When new restaurants are built, construction workers have contract jobs. Once the restaurant opens, there are vendors that supply each store with everything from food and soda to napkins and cleaning supplies.

Every new business creates a ripple effect in the economy; the bigger the business becomes, the larger the ripple. Bob Basham created many lucrative, successful ripples in his life. What ripples will you create?

MARY JANE, TILAPIA AND CATAMARANS

I interviewed Hans Geissler at his ten-acre aquaponics farm in Dade City, Florida. He was 73 at the time, thin as a rail and weathered. When I shook his hand, it felt gnarled and rough; it was the type of hand someone gets from building things and working hard.

The week before, Geissler had raced across the Gulf of Mexico in a catamaran he built 30 years ago. He won first place in a regatta against sailors half his age.

Even in his 70s, Geissler had amazing energy with a sparkle in his eye and laughter behind his accent. I got the sense he would live to be 100 years old, still sailing his catamaran through the gulf.

Geissler had ten siblings and grew up in Germany while WWII raged across Europe. One brother lost a leg in North Africa while driving a tank under the command of famed military strategist Erwin Rommel. Another spent three years in a Russian war camp until he escaped and returned to the family's hometown of Offenbach starving and covered with lice.

Wartime conditions in Germany were bleak, but the economy struggled for years after the war ceased. Geissler remembers always being hungry. His older siblings would come home to try and help the family get extra food and money, but the postwar years were still lean.

Once Geissler was old enough, he took up a plumbing apprenticeship. This trade not only taught him to work with his hands, but also built up his strength and confidence. In his spare time, Geissler was a heavy drinker and bare-knuckle brawler. He would go into bars with one of his brothers and take on fights for free beer.

Eventually, Geissler realized that free booze and a plumbing apprenticeship were hardly enough to keep him in work-starved Germany. He crossed into France and signed up for the French Foreign Legion.

At the time, French forces were still trying to control Algeria while

Algerian rebels fought for independence from colonial rule. The rebels hated the French occupiers so much that they would send children to roll live grenades into cafés where French Foreign Legion soldiers ate. The war was ruthless on both sides; the French government and the Algerian rebels were equally guilty of extreme violence and multiple massacres.

The Foreign Legion stationed Geissler at an outpost in the Sahara Desert where the Algerian days reached 120 degrees and nights hit 40-degree lows. His comrades were a combination of murderers, thieves and former Nazi officers. Any soldiers who abandoned their posts would be dragged back to base and violently beaten in front of the other men. Fortunately for Geissler, he suffered a severe back injury during a training exercise; the Foreign Legion sent him back to Germany less than a year after he became a Legionnaire.

When Geissler returned to Germany, he married his childhood sweetheart, Sigrid. He had two sisters who had married American soldiers and emigrated to the US, so when he was 23, he emigrated to America with Sigrid and spent the next few years working as a plumber and learning conversational English.

During the late 1960s, Geissler took up scuba diving and competitive spearfishing. He made a decent living from his plumbing operation, but he left it behind and instead started a catamaran-building business in 1973. His inventive vessels won competitions all over the world.

Eventually, Geissler began looking for funding to expand his business. Unfortunately, his solution to his problem was far from legal. He bought a 67-foot catamaran in Florida and sailed it to the Bahamas. With the help of a few smuggling partners, Geissler stripped the catamaran of all unnecessary equipment and furniture and loaded it with 14,000 pounds of the best Bahamian marijuana money could buy. The illegal cargo had a street value north of a million dollars. Geissler was an excellent sailor with extensive knowledge of the waterways along the East Coast. On paper, this shady transaction couldn't possibly go wrong.

The drop point was in Boston. Geissler was halfway there when he received a radio message that his Boston contact had been burned. Geissler quickly turned the boat around; he had another contact in Jacksonville who might buy his cargo.

A few hours later, a Coast Guard cutter crossed his path and radioed Geissler to ask about his point of origin and destination. The entire boat reeked of pot, but Geissler kept calm and told them he was transporting the boat from Baltimore to Miami. Miraculously, the cutter moved on and didn't take the time to board the catamaran.

To this day, Geissler is positive that if he hadn't turned his boat around, the Coast Guard would have boarded his vessel to take a closer look. Boats following a northern tack in the middle of the night were highly suspicious during those years. There was so much marijuana on that boat that the strong odor alone would have nailed him, and smuggling three tons worth of drugs would have landed Geissler in jail for the remainder of his life. Geissler's luck, however, was short-lived.

Geissler made it to Florida and offloaded his cargo, but he soon found himself in front of a judge for another smuggling indictment. Rather than try to deny what he'd done, Geissler told the judge that he was guilty. The judge subsequently sentenced Geissler to a nine-month stint at the maximum security prison in Lake Butler, Florida.

The men in prison were similar to the legionnaires: liars, rapists, thieves and murderers. The warden put Geissler to work fixing the old plumbing in the facility and working in the boiler room. It was at this point that Geissler began reading the Bible in earnest. An alcoholic guard monitoring the boiler room would not let him read the Bible, so Geissler approached the warden and asked to be reassigned to laundry duty. Here, the new guard let Geissler read scripture whenever Geissler had free time. Geissler pored over the Bible on a daily basis. He sought answers, peace, redemption and an escape from the lonely hours apart from his wife and family.

After Geissler served his sentence, he went back to building boats and became more active in his local church, going on mission trips to Central America and looking for a higher purpose in life. In the early '90s, he took a course in aquaculture through his parish and began thinking about sustainability. He contemplated how he could use this knowledge to help people in developing countries grow food in greater quantities.

While reading the Bible, Geissler realized that his calling was to teach others about faith and sustainability. He began conducting extensive research on both topics and learned how to combine hydroponics and aquaculture; this hybrid of two old technologies is known as aquaponics.

Aquaponics is the practice of raising fish and using the nitrogen from the fish waste to grow duckweed and assorted edible vegetables. With this technology, Geissler started a nonprofit organization called Morningstar Fishermen and has now established aquaponic farms all over the world. Today, people fly to Florida from other states and countries to learn how to build Geissler's sustainable aquaponics farms.

Geissler's life zigzagged in many directions, some more productive than others, but this seems to be the nature of the path for many entrepreneurs. Geissler made mistakes and paid dearly for them, but he was able to find a faith that made him realize his potential.

Hans Geissler found meaning by teaching people about sustainability and sharing his faith. Bob Basham found meaning in creating restaurant jobs for many people. Mary Kay Ash found meaning by helping women become independent business owners.

Profit is often an initial motivator for most folks who want to own a business, but a sense of purpose is even more important. Sure, people need money to build warehouses, buy equipment and obtain real estate, but purpose and meaning must be a top priority in any successful business.

LORD OF THE FLIES

Black soldier flies are commonly found in temperate climates worldwide. These harmless critters don't bite humans or spread disease, so most people have never heard of them. They mate in the hot summer months, lay eggs and then die. The little larvae are detritivorous, meaning, like earthworms, they eat organic waste like rotting vegetation and animal manure.

Black solider fly larvae contain high amounts of protein, so they're a terrific food source for many animals like pigs, lizards, chickens and shrimp. A farmer just needs good temperature regulation, precise humidity control and plenty of rotting vegetation to grow larvae. In a small space, a farmer could create lots of protein in a short amount of time. Even fecal waste from the fly larvae is valuable; it can be sold as nitrogen-rich plant fertilizer.

Glen Courtright, the founder of EnviroFlight, raises black soldier flies, harvests the eggs, hatches the larvae and sells the larvae as fish food. His Ohio-based facility is located near a brewery, so his larvae eat the spent grains from brewing beer. Before EnviroFlight, the brewery would have simply discarded the grains as waste. In some cases, companies even pay EnviroFlight to haul this waste material away from their facilities.

Unlike in other countries, there is a cultural taboo in the US against the consumption of insects, so most Americans won't see fly larvae sprinkled over a salad anytime soon, but it is more than adequate to feed our livestock. This is a healthier, more protein-rich alternative than using ground fish meal or grains to feed chickens, pigs and tilapia. The grub EnviroFlight sells can convert the nutrients in cast-off grains into protein and fertilizer, both of which are directly useful in agricultural endeavors.

Cultivating fly larvae does not require the slashing and burning of forests to create fields; it can be done vertically on ten-story buildings in the middle of densely-populated cities. The larvae can feed fish, which in turn can act as a food source for people. It takes far less energy and space to grow a pound of tilapia than a pound of beef.

Cows are endothermic mammals; they require tremendous amounts of clean water and acres of grass in order to reach a plate as a steak. Fish are exothermic and use far less energy to grow and thrive. People can raise tilapia in tanks. Tilapia require less water input than cattle when raised in a closed environment, and if the environment has a climate control system, you could condense any evaporated water and return it to the fish tanks.

The health benefits of eating fish are also debatably more advantageous than the ones that come from eating beef. Around the world, there exist several clusters of centenarians. These clusters are found in places like Okinawa, Sardinia, Nova Scotia and Icaria. These areas share two common traits: close proximity to the ocean and a diet rich in fish and fish oils.

As the global population grows, there will not be enough open grassland to meet the beef demands of the carnivorous middle class. The prices of beef, chicken and pork will rise; more people will move to fish as an alternative protein source, and the smart entrepreneurs who raise tilapia will profit. By extension, both aquaponics and soldier fly larvae will be important as the world looks at feeding the additional people who will populate this planet by 2050.

Brewer with EarthWorks, Geissler with Morningstar Fishermen and Courtright with EnviroFlight represent the environmental entrepreneurs of the future. They have invented local solutions for global challenges that use technology as it exists today. There are still technical issues that need finessing and government regulations to consider, but no one can deny the logic of what these entrepreneurs do. The folks who find a better way to help the world without destroying the environment will build huge companies with long lifespans.

THE $66 MILLION WOMAN

It was October of 2013. I was at Sony's Los Angeles studio pitching a business idea on the set of *Shark Tank*, an ABC reality television show. The shoot was early, and the producers kept handing me fresh cups of espresso. They asked me to be energetic when I pitched my business.

When I walked onto the stage and started my frenetic pitch, it was a bit surreal. After watching and studying the show for months, I was face-to-face with Mark Cuban, Kevin O'Leary, Lori Greiner, Robert Herjavec and Barbara Corcoran: a unique moment, to say the least.

After my pitch, Corcoran was the first to speak.

"I just have one question," Corcoran said. "Are you on drugs?"

My pitch went downhill from there.

I could hardly blame Corcoran for the question. Her no-nonsense attitude and direct nature likely stemmed from her tough journey to the top. Having lived through a volatile childhood, she was determined to control her adult life through business ownership rather than working for anyone else. She moved to Manhattan and started a real estate business with her boyfriend. Eventually, Corcoran split from her boyfriend and started a new real estate company. During this time, Corcoran raised her public profile by publishing The Corcoran Report, a brief on New York City real estate. She would send her report to all the local media outlets in the city. Reporters began calling Corcoran for quotes about the market, and this publicity helped grow her business.

As the Internet came into wide use, Corcoran started listing properties online. She pioneered the use of the Internet to reach a wider field of buyers and realized early on that if her team wasn't trying new things and failing, they were not innovating. She kept a suggestion box in her office and gave each agent a dollar per suggestion regardless of whether the suggestion worked or not. She built a culture where people were not afraid to fail; some of the best ideas came through failure.

In 2001, Corcoran sold her business for $66 million. Over the next decade, she worked as a columnist for several magazines, wrote many books and was a commentator on the *Today* show. She became a sought-after keynote speaker and real estate consultant.

Eventually, Corcoran started to appear on *Shark Tank* as one of the millionaire investors. At first the producers rejected her, but she insisted on a tryout with producer Mark Burnett to win her place on the show. Today, she is an investor in many businesses and has a net worth of about $80 million.

Like many famous media moguls, Barbara Corcoran made her first fortune with real estate, but then she wrote books and starred on television shows. She wasn't afraid to try new things and hated the idea of working for someone else. By raising her public profile, she was able to attract better salespeople to her company, and her local fame in New York City increased her chances of selling her business for a higher amount.

Growing and then selling a business is one successful strategy that many entrepreneurs use to create wealth, but some entrepreneurs use another time-proven strategy: taking an idea and selling franchises all over the country.

AN ELEPHANT AND 15 CRIMINALS

When I sat down to interview Marcus Price, he started by telling me that he always got his most brilliant ideas while on the loo.

"Along with some burning," Marcus added, "especially if I ate spicy chicken wings the night before."

Unfiltered, outrageous and shocking: these are classic Marcus Price traits. He has no filter and doesn't care what anyone thinks about it.

Marcus was born on Hope Street in the rough-and-tumble section of Cheltenham, England. His mother worked in a factory while his father built everything from cruise missile crates to custom trailers. His father was a bit of an 'Indiana Jones' character; he flew a microlight plane and sailed his boat far out into the Atlantic on a whim, sometimes going as far as North Africa.

During Marcus's school years, his father would pull him out of school for weeks at a time to go on wild adventures. On one trip, Marcus and his father were sailing far out in the North Atlantic when his father came down with a terrible toothache. His father drank whiskey to dull the ache and then asked Marcus to take the helm.

"I have to lay down for a few hours," Marcus's father said. "See that constellation to the north? Steer in that direction until the sun comes up." Marcus's father fostered his son's independent spirit from a young age, helping Marcus to become an early entrepreneur.

When Marcus was 5, his father bought him a box of foam earplugs and took him to the local airport. While his father was busy flying over Cheltenham, little Marcus was back at the hangar selling earplugs to pilots for a decent profit.

The foam earplugs were just the beginning of Marcus's business career. When he was 7, he went with his friends to the roughest pubs in Cheltenham and sang Christmas carols to all the bar patrons, even bringing along his 3-year-old brother for an added cuteness factor. The patrons would tip him outrageously well.

When Marcus was 8, he bought a pregnant mouse, gave it plenty of food and before long had dozens of mice. He put them in cardboard boxes and sold them to his schoolmates.

Then, at the age of 12, Marcus started buying office supplies to sell to the teachers at school. He eventually graduated to peddling candy bars and soda to the other kids. Marcus sometimes hauled 40 pounds of inventory to school. Occasionally, bullies would steal his money or products, but Marcus considered that the cost of doing business.

"All I needed was something to sell, and my income could stretch to infinity," Marcus said. "Working an hourly job was limited; selling was far more lucrative."

Marcus also realized the importance of competence. "I just had to do things better than 95 percent of my competitors."

As a young man, Marcus harbored big dreams. He wanted to be rich, a pilot and an American. He saw the United States as a place with no limits, unlike England where you were born into the working class and stayed there for life. He had seen neighbors work at the same factories and drink at the same pubs every night only to retire from those factories as old, broken alcoholics.

Unfortunately, at 19, Marcus found himself working at a paper mill. It was a dark, dangerous place where he could tell the age of the workers by how many fingers they were missing.

"If you lost an arm on the factory floor, you might even get promoted to a desk job and get off the night shift," Marcus recalled.

The owners of the paper factory owned the entire village surrounding it, from the housing units and the pub to the bus that brought workers to the factory gate like clockwork. It was the exact opposite of where Marcus wanted to be.

One Monday afternoon, Marcus was walking past a travel agency in Cheltenham and saw an ad in the window. It read, "Tickets to Orlando, Florida, Only £99!" The tickets were only available for a flight that Thursday, so Marcus went to work and tried to convince his friend, John, to join him.

"I can't just leave," John protested. "We have to plan; I have an upcoming court date for a speeding ticket."

In every person's life, there is at least one moment when a seemingly small decision can drastically change the course of events. For Marcus, this decision involved selling most of his possessions to make that flight to Orlando, leaving John behind to toil at the factory and pay his tickets.

Marcus got off his flight in Orlando late that evening and walked to the nearest Denny's for his first meal in America. To his amazement, he could order eggs late at night, which was unheard of in England.

"What a country," Marcus marveled. "So many choices!"

Marcus booked a room in a cheap hotel, woke the next morning and determined that he would set out across America. Marcus had taken up skydiving back in England, so he had packed a full parachute, cooking pans, camping gear, clothes and a small kettle for brewing tea. As he walked along the road leaving Orlando, he started to chuck his heaviest gear, but he kept the kettle.

"Over the next few years, I would find myself broke and homeless many times in America, and sometimes just brewing a cup of tea was the only thing that kept me sane."

At one point, the traveling circus came through town, and Marcus decided to travel with them for a few weeks as a laborer.

"The workers were angry white guys fleeing arrest warrants, drunk Indians and random Mexicans. We could put up the Big Top in 20 minutes using one elephant and 15 criminals."

In the early '90s, there was an underground culture of skydivers, party maniacs and itinerant foreigners floating around the small skydiving airports across North America. These people lived in tents and converted vans, traveled with the seasons and supported themselves through off-the-grid living and packing parachutes for cash. The wild scene Marcus found at Zephyr Hills Airport was a ragtag group of people from all over the world who brewed their own alcohol and cleverly dodged the immigration authorities.

Here, Marcus put up a small sign advertising services as a parachute packer. His first customer approached him and asked how much experience he had packing parachutes.

Marcus was honest. "I don't really know how to do it, but if you teach me, I'll work cheap." This customer actually taught him how to properly pack a parachute. For the next week, Marcus worked for that customer.

After that first gig, Marcus was able to get steady work as a packer. Because he lived in a tent with no other responsibilities, his cash income was enough to keep him afloat. It was then that Marcus realized a fundamental truth.

"It all comes down to having the balls to ask for help," Marcus said. "If you stick your neck out, somebody will always rescue you."

As Marcus traveled around the skydiving circuit, he bought a camera and started jumping out of planes to film skydiving clients. This created the need for a more secure place than a canvas tent to keep his increasingly expensive electronic equipment. At a vehicle auction, Marcus purchased an old city bus for $2,000.

"[The bus] had no fuel gauge," Marcus remembered, "and I wondered why until I went to gas it up and discovered the tank held 250 gallons of diesel. Apparently, the city just topped it off each day, so it never reached empty."

Marcus ripped out the old bus's seats and turned it into his home and mobile editing studio. Over the next few years, he would drive the bus across the country to follow the skydiving seasons. To date, he has clocked over 4,000 successful jumps out of perfectly good airplanes.

In the summer of 1997, Marcus was working in upstate New York when a brilliant young woman named M.J. came out of an airport to skydive. They started talking, and M.J. returned the following week to move in with Marcus. Marcus had finally met his match; M.J. was just as much of a free spirit as Marcus and had a brain to match his. A year later, M.J. and Marcus got married and are still happily married today. Being the practical problem solvers that they've always been, Marcus and M.J. passed on an extravagant honeymoon in order to buy better editing computers for their video business.

In the first years of marriage, Marcus and M.J. tried out many types of businesses. Marcus learned how to build websites, opened an Internet café, sold tie-dye clothing and started an online store for skydiving equipment. Marcus had always dreamed of becoming a commercial pilot, so he eventually went to flight school to fly jetliners.

The terrorist attacks happened on September 11th of that year.

After 9/11, the bottom dropped out of the commercial airline business. The FAA blocked all foreign-born pilots from earning a jet rating, limiting Marcus to a commercial job flying only propeller-driven planes. Dejected, Marcus quit pilot school and went back to Zephyr Hills to regroup.

While in pilot school, Marcus and M.J. had maintained a modest online mail-order business that sold skydiving equipment. They noticed that there were no convenient places to locally mail packages, so they decided to open a small store in an empty retail space in Zephyr Hills. They named the store Goin' Postal, and after the first 18 months in business, they had grossed over $200,000 with a profit margin of 25 percent.

Over the next few years, Marcus traveled the country to sell Goin' Postal franchises across four time zones. The rest, as they say, is history.

Goin' Postal now has over 250 locations, though it's hardly Marcus's last project. As of 2017, Marcus is working on a new real estate franchise as well. Like any good entrepreneur, he has to keep moving, experimenting and trying new ideas.

DRAWING CATS

Steve Gadlin wants to draw a cat for you. He will take most requests; a drawing might feature a husband and wife as cats celebrating an anniversary, a cat watching a beloved sports team or even a cat riding a rainbow unicorn. It costs $9.95 per drawing, and Steve has inked over 17,600 pieces of cat art to date.

When Gadlin appeared on *Shark Tank*, he did a little dance and sang his theme song. This was enough for billionaire investor Mark Cuban; he bought 32 percent of Gadlin's company for a cool $25,000.

Gadlin started the business, "as a hobby, a side project, a joke among friends." After the national exposure from *Shark Tank*, Gadlin's business generated over $180,000 in revenue.

During all this, Gadlin never quit his Chicago-based day job working for a television station as a web developer. I Want to Draw a Cat for You was just one of several creative side businesses Gadlin started on nights and weekends. Most recently, Gadlin raised over $20,000 on Kickstarter for his next project, a unique talent show called *Starmakers*.

There is a myth that people have to leave their full-time jobs and mortgage their houses to start businesses. Nothing is further from the truth. Gadlin is a perfect example of someone with a full-time job who used his creativity and spare time to have fun and create revenue. In doing so, he has become a blogger, marketer, SEO expert and famous entrepreneur.

You don't have to go broke to become an entrepreneur. Start small.

I Want to Draw a Cat for You was a fad, something that launched, hit a specific apex and faded in popularity. Gadlin generated tens of thousands of dollars in revenue and made a tidy profit off that amount. His total expenses for his business amounted to the cost of paper, postage, markers, a website and his time spent drawing cats. The physical limitation to his business was the fact that Gadlin had to generate all the drawings himself, but other than that, it was a great example of a goofy idea turned into some serious money.

Gadlin's business did not require rooms full of expensive inventory, a pricey building or even heavy advertising costs. He could run that entire operation on a shoestring budget. His only risk was the cost of the website and looking silly on television.

I Want to Draw a Cat for You will never be a billion-dollar enterprise, but it serves as a fantastic example of creative entrepreneurship. It created revenue from nothing save for a silly idea that was born out of nooks and crannies in Gadlin's mind.

FISHING ON WEDNESDAY

In 2003, I started a little company called Balloon Distractions. I sent balloon twisters out to family-friendly restaurants, and the restaurants paid us a fee. The business is an ongoing enterprise to this day, with teams working in restaurants in major markets across the United States.

I hesitated to include Balloon Distractions in this book because it's so small as compared to billion-dollar companies like KFC, Mary Kay or Outback Steakhouse. In its best year, Balloon Distractions filled 10,000 bookings and generated $750,000 in gross revenue. From 2003 to 2016, Balloon Distractions generated $7 million in lifetime revenue, classifying it as a small business. In an $80 trillion global economy, my balloon business is barely a drop of water, but even a small business can give its owner a nice lifestyle and many options.

Because of Balloon Distractions, rich folks yelled at me on national television. If I had worked a normal job, my *Shark Tank* appearance would never have happened.

Balloon Distractions trainers have taught over 5,000 people to twist balloons and earn a great part-time income since 2003. Most Balloon Distractions entertainers are high school and college kids; both of my teenaged daughters began working for Balloon Distractions when they turned 16.

Owning Balloon Distractions gave me the freedom to live my life on my schedule without answering to a boss or larger corporate structure. When my daughters were in elementary school, I could bring them to lunch on a Tuesday afternoon while wearing shorts, a t-shirt and flip flops.

I learned a ton about how to lead a team, build systems, design a compensation plan and do hundreds of other small things that entrepreneurs have to learn along the way. Even 14 years later, I'm still learning new ways to run my company.

I traveled around the country and built teams in places like Seattle, Los Angeles, Minneapolis, Charlotte and Atlanta. I got to work with some wonderful people over all these years. People who entertain kids tend to be creative minds with big hearts.

Sometimes I take my freedom for granted; recently, I went fishing on the Gulf of Mexico with my friend, Jason. Jason works in the offshore oil business and spends 30 days on the rig working 12-hour shifts. He then comes home for 30 days off. Jason earns a great income, but I can't imagine being locked up on a ship for half the year. In my mind, it's not worth it.

If someone were to design a business around residual income, that person could go fishing on any day of the week, even Wednesdays when other folks are busy and the pond is delightfully free of other hobby fishermen. That person could design his or her life in a million possible ways, take time back and leave the humdrum corporate world.

For this reason, I started a second business in 2014 with a leadership and financial coaching company called Life Leadership. Life Leadership operates in similar ways to Mary Kay, allowing anyone to inexpensively start a company. The Life business model was attractive because it sells personal and professional development material in 15 countries around the world. Balloon Distractions, on the other hand, has always been limited to the United States. I liked the idea of a business with a global scale, but I did not want to start another business from scratch.

Both Life Leadership and Balloon Distractions provide a monthly income for me and my family. These businesses allowed me the free time to write books like this one. I've also used the teachings in the Life business to increase the profitability of Balloon Distractions.

In 2017 I got involved in the solar business in Tampa. I had the flexibility to do this because of the base income I had developed from my other businesses. In 2018 I started a YouTube channel called "The Solar Nerd". This will probably grow into my next stream of income.

Everyone is different and has been blessed with unique skills and gifts. Some people were meant to build huge businesses, and others were meant to start nonprofit organizations like my buddy Hans Geissler. Some will fail repeatedly like Harland Sanders only to stay persistent and find success later in life.

I was 29 when I became a full-time entrepreneur and 40 when I published my first book. I was 43 when I got into the solar biz.

Bob Basham was in his 60s when he started a new restaurant chain. Ray Kroc was 52 when he started selling McDonald's franchises. Barbara Corcoran was 64 when she landed her role on Shark Tank. Hans Geissler was 40 years old when he went to jail and found his faith.

There are many seasons in life and many roles that you will play across those seasons. Part of the excitement in life is being open to new ideas and trying new things; age doesn't really matter. One of the sure signs you are on the right path is when you enjoy whatever it is that you're doing.

Some of the skills you learn in the eraly part of your life will become vital to your success later on, my work with Balloon Distractions made it easier to sell over 2 million dollars in solar my first year in that new business.

If you are unhappy with where you are right now, you can learn something new and make some changes in your life. You have the freedom to try new things; you don't have to be tied to your job or life situation forever. If you can't go fishing on Wednesday and you want to have that freedom, you might need to get uncomfortable and try something different. When you find yourself in this situation, the only bad decision is no decision at all.

DARK MOTIVES

There are many reasons people become entrepreneurs; some folks prefer working for themselves and controlling their schedules. Others start businesses because they see unmet needs in their communities.

Some entrepreneurs have a darker motive when launching a new idea. In 1997, film producer Joe Francis launched the *Girls Gone Wild* series. Over the next ten years, his team produced 83 videos and generated tens of millions of dollars in revenue on the backs of exploited women.

The videos featured intoxicated college women who took off their clothing for the camera and did things they probably regretted later in life. Like any business that took advantage of the worst part of human nature, *Girls Gone Wild* had a few years of success only to quickly crash and burn.

By 2007, Joe Francis was facing criminal charges that ranged from soliciting a prostitute to tax evasion. His company went bankrupt in 2013 and he's now hiding in Mexico to evade jail time in the US.

If the needle on your moral compass is spinning around wildly, you will never enjoy long-term success. You might be able to lie, cheat and steal for a little while, but those decisions will come back in spades. These won't be the pretty spades like on a deck of cards; instead, they'll be rusty iron spades used to dig up dirt and innuendo to throw on your coffin of a reputation.

If you start a business that has a negative impact on the universe, you will eventually experience the same karmic retribution that ruined Francis's life. This could be a strip club, liquor store chain or even a website that promotes adult content. Whatever business you decide to build should have motives that are good and noble in order to attract better people to the business. These people will not only be customers, but also possibly team members who will help take the business to the next level.

Integrity and rock-solid character are important no matter what your situation might be. It's better to run an honest business that does $50,000 per year than a dishonest one that does $500,000 that same year.

The honest business can continue to grow for the next 20 years, while the dishonest business will send its owner to prison. There is an entire government infrastructure in place to punish dishonest operators that includes law enforcement, health and labor regulators and a federal taxing authority.

Before anyone makes a dollar, that person should consider the motive behind his or her business and swear to only get ahead by working hard and being creative. It is important to make sure that everything an entrepreneur does or says in business is legal, moral and ethical.

Francis saw a huge short-term gain in starting *Girls Gone Wild* but knew from the beginning that it was a shady enterprise. He didn't care and paid dearly for his recklessness. Many ideas with darker motives might also look profitable for the first few years, but when considering a new concept, it makes sense to ask a few questions:

1. Does this business take advantage of the darker side of human nature?
2. Would I want to let my own children work in this business?
3. Would I be ashamed to tell my friends and neighbors about it?

It pays to work in a great business with noble motives and an honest product. People feel better about themselves and have pride in their work when they do this. They feel good about who they represent and won't lose sleep at night.

There is an old cliché about nice guys finishing last. By and large, this simply doesn't ring true in business. The entrepreneurs who run companies that serve customers with respect will finish first, and any business that does not treat the public with kindness will inevitably face failure.

YOUR TRILLION-DOLLAR BUSINESS

What do Google, Facebook, Uber, PayPal, Airbnb and eBay all have in common?

All of these companies do nothing more than move information. Uber does not own a fleet of cars (yet), Airbnb does not own a hotel and eBay does not own any inventory. Each of these companies move information in ways that create profit.

Over the next 30 years, there will be countless companies that capture audiences in the information space, spreading globally and growing much faster than traditional businesses with brick-and-mortar stores.

The prime real estate of the future resides in people's pockets on their smartphones. The largest companies of the future will exist as apps on phones; this is why Facebook was in such a rush to capture that real estate in 2010. This is why Mark Zuckerberg enjoys a net worth in excess of $50 billion today.

Business concepts that require a physical location (like restaurants) will still be necessary, but they will not expand nearly as quickly as information businesses that identify and fill a need for everyone on the planet.

The trillion-dollar information business of the future might even have a strange name like Snapchat, Etsy, Pinterest, GitHub or Xiaomi. Finding and establishing that global brand is what millions of entrepreneurs are trying to do each day; the companies mentioned in this chapter only scrape the surface. The only limits on these ideas are the human imagination and the number of users willing to download an app.

For every huge information company that exists, there will be thousands of smaller opportunities for information concepts that serve more specific niches. When I recently purchased a used car, the salesperson handed me a Carfax report on the vehicle. This useful report showed where the owner initially purchased the vehicle, whether the vehicle had been in any accidents and the mileage of the vehicle at each service interval. From looking at the report, I could see that the previous owner had maintained the car at proper intervals and driven the car about 15,000 miles per year. This indicated that it probably had more highway use and less wear-and-tear on the vehicle. I could buy with confidence.

Carfax started in 1984 as a mileage reporting service for used car buyers in North America. The company grew slowly prior to the Internet, then much faster after 2001. Used car buyers can ask for a Carfax report on any used vehicle they are considering. The dealerships pay a small fee per report, and the report allows more transparency in the sales process. The Carfax report makes it more difficult to sell a car that has sustained frame damage or was stuck in a flood. It also prevents dishonest car dealers from rolling back odometers on used vehicles; if someone is looking at a used Camry with 45,000 miles on it and the Carfax shows an oil change last month at 75,000 miles, that person might want to shop elsewhere. Because many buyers now request Carfax reports, any dealer that does not supply them loses market share; Carfax has positioned itself as a must-have service. As a company, Carfax is lean and profitable with less than 800 employees generating $400 million in revenue. Carfax doesn't need a manufacturing facility, warehouses or retail space; no one can steal, lose or damage the product.

Nonprofit organizations are also using information technology to expand. In 2005, then-couple Jessica Jackley and Matt Flannery launched Kiva in San Francisco. Kiva is a nonprofit organization that loans out small amounts of money to entrepreneurs in developing countries to help them start or maintain businesses. Kiva allows anyone to create an account and lend money to someone else on the other side of the world. At this moment, Kiva has loaned out over $745 million to some of the poorest people in the world with an impressive 98 percent repayment rate. This new niche (known as microfinance) gives people who are well below the poverty line access to loans and banking. Kiva is a perfect example of entrepreneurs who leveraged the movement of information to make the world a better place.

What new information business could someone put together to serve clients? Carfax brought more honesty and transparency to the car buying process. Kiva put millions of dollars in the hands of entrepreneurs abroad. What idea can you create that uses information to benefit humanity?

BOOMS AND BUSTS

A discussion about entrepreneurship would be incomplete if I left out the effects of booms and busts on the worldwide economy. There are many variables that make the economy grow and shrink. Adoption of a new technology, unrest in countries with crucial resources or natural disasters could affect the economy in ways that impact entrepreneurs.

The discovery of vast natural gas deposits in the Marcellus Shale changed the global energy equation and lowered the cost of fossil fuels in North America. Natural gas generates 27 percent of the electricity for the three main power grids in the United States; coal generates 39 percent. Just ten years ago, coal represented almost 50 percent of the domestic energy generation for the United States, so the increase in natural gas led to a decrease in domestic demand for coal. The boom in natural gas represented billions of dollars in opportunity for those connected to that industry.

During the frenzied dot-com boom in 1999, many Silicon Valley tech companies with zero sales and no tangible product went public and raised tens of millions of dollars. These companies had no shortage of clever ideas, but they took investors' money before proving the ideas in the marketplace. Some of these tech companies used funds to build huge offices with ping pong tables and video game rooms for employees. The CEOs would talk about the 'burn rate' of investors' dollars, and in many cases, all the investors' capital went towards frills and inflated salaries; when these companies went out of business, the investors lost everything.

As the saying goes, "a fool and his gold are soon parted." In the case of investors who bought shares in tech companies with no sales and no product, this adage applies. Greed and stupidity are always contributing factors when economic bubbles pop; those who fail to perform due diligence on investments are far more likely to lose their fortunes.

The example above implies that booms and busts only impact big-time investors rolling in dough, but this is far from true. If you are working a traditional job to support a family, you could be even more vulnerable to the boom and bust cycle. This is yet another reason to pay off debt and generate an additional stream of income through a side business.

Sometimes booms can create unforeseen consequences. During the late 1990s tech boom, several companies built a fiber optic cable network underneath the oceans between Europe, Asia and North America. The initial investors lost money when the market corrected and those fiber optic companies failed, but the installation led to faster global Internet capabilities and the outsourcing of customer service operations to India and the Philippines. In 1990, a long-distance call from New York to Tokyo was 60 cents per minute. Fiber optics reduced that price tenfold by the year 2000. The next time you find yourself on the phone with a telemarketer in Calcutta, you can thank the '90s tech boom.

Unrealistic valuations in a specific segment of the economy are a clear sign of a boom that is about to bust. History has repeated itself over and over again in this regard; for example, tulip mania in the 1600s caused the price of tulips to go sky high.

Real estate has also had many boom and bust cycles in the last century. During the last boom in 2006, I watched neighbors sell their homes at a gain to buy bigger homes that were equally inflated in price. The market corrected itself in 2008, and home prices went back down to where they should have been all along.

I still live in the same home that I purchased in a slow market in 2003. The real estate bust had zero effect on my personal finances. If you refuse to participate in a boom, you are less likely to suffer when the boom turns sour.

There were investors who stockpiled funds on the sidelines during the housing boom; when prices finally corrected, those investors bought many homes at steep discounts and flourished. The investors who sustain the greatest damage during a boom are those who borrow money to buy that hot commodity of the moment. That commodity could be tech stocks, tulips or townhouses; when the bust happens, those investors accrue massive debt even after selling the commodity that sunk them in the first place.

Cash is king; debt is cancer. If you are worried that you might be in the middle of a boom market, you will want to start converting those gains back to cash. Even if an individual misses out on some of the gains at the tail end of the boom, he or she will be able to prevent personal catastrophe when everything quickly busts.

There is always a cause-and-effect chain of events behind booms and busts. Between now and 2024, fossil fuel costs will reach a price point that raises utility electric costs as well as the price of gasoline. The rising costs of manufacturing gasoline combined with the lowered cost of creating solar energy, better electric cars and more efficient battery technology create the formula for a huge boom in green technology. Entrepreneurs like Elon Musk are already preparing for this with phenomenal Tesla electric vehicles and Solar City.

Outside of the green tech boom, there will be a vast market in developed nations for services that serve the elderly. By some estimates, the average American lifespan by 2050 will be 86 years. The companies that meet the impending housing and medical needs of this aging population will do well.

YOU CAN WRITE YOUR STORY

The common thread that runs through the lives of all the entrepreneurs in this book is one of creativity, vision, action and persistence over a long period of time. Most entrepreneurs never could have predicted the twists and turns that would eventually lead them to fortune.

When someone becomes old and gray, all that person will have is a story; those who embrace some form of entrepreneurship normally have a more interesting story than others.

There is nothing wrong with working hard in a traditional job, paying the bills and taking care of a family. This is a noble and honorable thing to do. Imagine, though, if someone veered away from the average path and became more of an adventure-seeking entrepreneur.

Many of the entrepreneurs in this book started out in various odd jobs and followed a meandering path before striking out on their own. This is how most successful business owners eventually find their craft. You can take what you learned in a traditional job and apply it to a business, but you will need to learn additional skills, too.

Business owners will face rejection, obstacles and frequent frustration, but they will also meet new people and create results that never would have happened had they never made the attempt. They will learn, grow and become much more interesting.

Take action and try something. Every entrepreneur who ever made it big tried and failed many times, but these successful people got back up and kept going.

All people, regardless of age, have something to offer the world: positive ideas that have yet to be realized. God did not put people on this planet to be average. As long as you have a pulse, you have the potential to write some exciting life chapters. You story is not over until you are.

WHY NOW?

Someone who takes the risk to go out and start a new business invariably creates opportunity and jobs all around them, from the employees of the new business to the vendors and suppliers that make that business possible. According to *The Economist*, one person who becomes a billionaire creates at least 10,000 jobs.

Harland Sanders, Mary Kay Ash and Bob Basham created global companies that employ millions of people and will continue to create jobs and opportunity for decades.

Without entrepreneurs, there is less economic growth, innovation and competition. Even the largest businesses in the world such as IBM and Microsoft started as small ventures between a few people.

A new business is small and nimble; it can take risks and make mistakes. If the original business plan is not working, the business owner can experiment until he or she finds a better way to make a larger profit.

There is also a strong connection between entrepreneurship and leadership in capitalistic society. Successful entrepreneurs have influence and wealth that can be used to benefit society. Bill Gates and Warren Buffet have both pledged their wealth to making the world a better place.

The Gates Foundation has almost eliminated polio from the face of the planet. If Bill Gates had not become an entrepreneur, he would not have been able to spearhead this cause and save countless lives.

As a member of Rotary International, I saw firsthand how local entrepreneurs and business owners stepped up and took leadership in our community. Entrepreneurs are comfortable with taking an initial idea, making a plan, recruiting a team and bringing that idea to life. Entrepreneurs are people of action who don't need to be told what to do; they simply do it.

MARCUS LEMONIS

I normally wouldn't recommend that people watch reality television to learn about business, but an exception to this rule is the hit show *The Profit* with Marcus Lemonis. Watching Lemonis step into various businesses to improve margins can teach anyone some basic business principles. Unlike most reality stars, Lemonis is someone of integrity who is motivated to help people no matter what their challenges may be.

Lemonis was born in Lebanon before an American couple adopted him and took him to Miami. In his early years, he moved up rapidly in his family's automotive business before transitioning into a leadership position at Camping World. He became CEO in 2011 and is currently worth $2 billion.

Lemonis's entire business philosophy focuses on the improvement of people, process and product. In *The Profit*, Lemonis takes his expertise from running a billion-dollar business and works with struggling business owners who need help in these areas. In some cases, Lemonis walks into a business that is drowning in debt and saves the owners from bankruptcy by cutting costs and improving the operational side of the company.

Lemonis visits each business, identifies opportunities for greater profits and implements the needed changes to make success happen. Lemonis doesn't just make smart recommendations; he also puts his own cash on the line by buying a percentage of each business.

Inevitably, there's always some reality show drama included in the mix; in many cases, Lemonis has to deal with the ego and stubbornness of the failing business owner. Sometimes, Lemonis can't get through to the business owner and walks away from the deal. After watching a few episodes, anyone would be amazed at the stupidity of the people who resist Lemonis's ideas; after all, he does this for a living. It's crazy that some folks (who ask Lemonis for help in the first place) still ignore and sometimes belittle Lemonis's plans to make their business successful.

The best part of the show is watching how Lemonis wraps his brain around a dysfunctional business by building on what works and fixing what doesn't. *The Profit* teaches the basics of everyday operations and troubleshooting. For those who want to be successful entrepreneurs, this is an excellent (albeit unorthodox) beginning resource.

YOUR MOST VALUABLE ASSET

You're already miles ahead of those who don't read or have no desire to get ahead in life if you've read this far into this book. After all, your mind is the most valuable asset you own.

Without a brain, you are a useless bag of meat. The brain is key to every triumph and failure. The biggest difference between a billionaire and someone who fails in life is the quality of thinking in the crucial six inches between their ears. We all have the same 24 hours in each day, but winners and losers see the world differently and act accordingly.

You can start a great system of improvement by clearing off a shelf and creating a small library of paperback books. I have my own small list of favorites that can be purchased for a few bucks online.

1. *Rich Dad Poor Dad* by Robert Kiyosaki
2. *Launching a Leadership Revolution* by Orrin Woodward
3. *How to Win Friends and Influence People* by Dale Carnegie
4. *The Magic of Thinking Big* by David J. Schwartz
5. *The Inevitable* by Kevin Kelly
6. *Personality Plus* by Florence Littauer
7. *How I Raised Myself from Failure to Success* by Frank Bettger
8. *Abundance* by Peter H. Diamandis
9. *The Psychology of Winning* by Denis Waitley
10. *Financial Fitness* by Orrin Woodward and Chris Brady

Reading through these books can get you interested in other material and into a daily reading habit that can help develop a millionaire mindset. It all starts in the brain; thoughts lead to actions, actions lead to results and results lead to fortune.

A hundred bucks spent on books might motivate you to start a business that creates opportunity for thousands of other people.

Think about the return on that investment.

You will finish 30 to 40 books per year if you read for 15 minutes a day. I have read well over 2,000 books in my life; this gave me a better foundation as an entrepreneur, writer, and human being. Reading those books over the last 25 years was time well spent.

Reading books makes an entrepreneur more effective with teams, vendors and clients. Start the learning process now before starting a business.

THE IMPORTANCE OF MENTORS

Every business contains countless small details that entrepreneurs won't learn about until they are in the thick of things. You can spend ages trying to figure out the lay of the land on your own or seek out a mentor who has already blazed a trail in that industry to save yourself a lot of time and effort. As profiled in a previous chapter, Marcus Lemonis is not just an investor but also a mentor to business owners.

The right mentor can help you overcome nearly any challenge. If you are overweight, find a mentor who has lost 100 pounds and ask him or her about how they did it. If you are an alcoholic, you can attend an Alcoholics Anonymous meeting and learn how to achieve sobriety from people who have already done it. If you want a great marriage, seek out a mentor whose marriage has lasted for 50 years.

The honesty and integrity of your mentor is crucial; anyone can find a mentor who runs the local crime syndicate and learn how to steal cars, bribe local officials and break kneecaps. On the flip side, anyone can also find a mentor of integrity who follows the rules and derives profit honestly without trying to cheat the system. If you live in a place rife with corruption, you must be careful not to learn the wrong habits from the wrong people.

It doesn't take long to plug into a network of successful people who get together to benefit from positive association with each other. Successful people know that it takes a large network to make it big, so they are always in the center of the action, shaking hands, making conversation and getting to know people.

When I wanted to get into the solar business, I sought out and built a friendship with Steve Ruthersford, the owner of Tampa Bay Solar. I had to be humble enough to seek him out and ask him to teach me that industry.

When meeting a possible mentor, offer to buy him or her a coffee and be upfront about seeking a mentor. This is never an acceptable time to ask for a job, favor or loan. The right mentor has a desire to help people. Truly successful people realize the importance of paying it forward and helping other people to do the same.

Remember those who helped you and be open to becoming a mentor to others when you reach a certain level of success.

SYSTEMS MATTER

There are complex interconnected systems spinning all around the human body; right now, blood cells are picking up oxygen in my lungs and transporting it to my brain. Electrons are bouncing off this page, and the human eye receives them and transports their 'message' to the brain via signals moving along the optic nerve. The brain then processes these signals into meaning.

There's a system at work on the outdoor orchid shelf at my home here in Florida. Small lizards, tree frogs and various insects live among the 30 species of orchids on the shelf. The orchids attract small insects; lizards and frogs then eat those bugs. The nitrogen-rich waste from the critters fertilizes the orchid roots, and I enjoy the blooming orchids with my daughters. An entire connected ecosystem of plants and animals lives on that little shelf; all I have to do is add water on a weekly basis.

Complex systems are found outside of nature, too. Look at the simple chair on which you may be sitting while reading this book. There was an entire manufacturing and distribution system in place to get that chair underneath you. Someone sourced metal and wood to bring those to the factory that bolted the chair together. A distributor transported the chair from the factory to the retailer who then sold it to the customer.

A well-designed system takes something that is complex and makes it appear simple. In many cases, these systems are invisible most people until they fail; when that happens, you will notice them right away. Very few people give any thought to the electric grid until a storm knocks out power and you have to live through a few days with no refrigeration, lights or air conditioning.

The last few chapters of this book will focus on the various business models available to entrepreneurs, but an awareness of the importance of interconnected systems is key to understanding these models.

Any successful business is just a set of clever systems that work together to create profit for the owner. McDonald's is a billion-dollar business because Ray Kroc and his team invented foolproof systems that eliminated the lengthy trial-and-error process found in most traditional businesses.

Within Balloon Distractions, I had to create several systems from scratch: online training modules, an Internet-based scheduler and a billing system that makes sure clients pay on time. These systems saved time and utilized technology to the company's benefit, allowing Balloon Distractions to fill over 120,000 bookings across the country since 2003.

Look at every complex process and consider how a system can simplify it. It may take time and effort to implement a new system and might be a huge pain in the moment, but it's worth it in the long run. Functional systems allow entrepreneurs to focus on growing the business instead of merely running it.

Even as I'm writing this book on my computer, I can take a break to monitor the cash flow from Balloon Distractions, look at the sales for my first book or track the volume running through my Life business. These systems are in place to help me grow each of my endeavors accordingly.

Each business represents a separate stream of income that will grow with little additional investment on my behalf. I'm using the systems in Life Leadership to generate a residual profit. If 10,000 people go on Amazon and download my first book, *We Twist for Tips*, there is nothing else I need to do to facilitate that transaction. Amazon will simply deposit the commission in my bank account next week.

There is no need to reinvent the wheel. You don't need to be a software genius; you can benefit from using a system that someone else already built. This is way easier than inventing a new system from scratch.

If you have talent as a coder, you can improve an existing system and build a business from that. Just a small tweak to a system that improves margins by 1 percent across a global marketplace could be worth billions of dollars to the entrepreneur or business that makes it happen.

Take a moment to consider all the systems that people use in their jobs, businesses or nonprofit organizations. Note the systems that are quietly buzzing along to make it easier for a consumer to use a product or service.

Consider the systems that can work for you as an entrepreneur. Think about how the right systems can simplify a business. Conversely, think about how a lack of systems can hold you back and erode your profitability.

START WITH SALES

I visited the local Mercedes-Benz dealership and ran into my friend, Jay. Jay has been a car salesman for a few years and told me how he earned $33,000 in his best month. Jay has never owned a business, but he gets to determine the size of his income within the larger entity of the dealership. Jay does not have to pay rent on the building or place ads in the paper; his role is to help people move through the sales process.

My oldest daughter, Claire, took a sales job at a local jewelry store when she was a freshman in college. They pay her an hourly wage plus a percentage on commissions.

Both Jay and Claire are professionals with plenty of charm and a great knowledge of their products. They are employees with the ability to double or triple their income by strategically reaching out to customers. In sales parlance, both Jay and Claire 'eat what they kill'.

On any sales team, there are people who earn $40,000 per year working next to others who earn $40,000 per month. Aside from lawyers, doctors and business owners, salespeople have the potential to earn far more than people in other professions.

If you are interested in business ownership, it would be wise to first take a job in sales. All good entrepreneurs have sales skills; if you can't sell a product or service, you'll have a hard time launching any type of successful business.

Some folks harbor negative stereotypes about salespeople. They think a person has to be pushy, seedy or obnoxious to succeed in sales, but this is far from true. Successful salespeople generally have excellent listening skills, an understanding of product and talents in communicating well with people.

Every business owner highlighted in this book had to succeed at sales in order to promote a business. Marcus Price and Bob Basham sell franchises; Mary Kay Ash and Harland Sanders sell products like makeup and fried chicken recipes. Every page of this book is selling the reader on the idea of flipping to the next page instead of chucking the entire book out the window. As a business owner, I sell my team on the idea of following my lead. I sell restaurants on the idea of latex entertainment.

Think about every teen who has ever talked his or her parents into ignoring a curfew. Think about successfully asking someone on a date or asking someone to get married. Selling is something that happens in almost every human interaction, even if no money is changing hands.

There is no voodoo magic behind selling; it breaks down to a few simple steps:

1. Make a friend.
2. Find a need or want.
3. Present a solution to that need.
4. Ask the friend to buy.

I sold over 450 Toyota vehicles from 2001 to 2003. Many families bought not just one, but two cars from me in a 24-month period. In truth, I wasn't selling cars; I was selling solutions to a want or need.

The guy who bought a Prius needed transportation, but wanted a green solution. The mom with five kids who bought a minivan wanted a reliable, comfortable way to transport her brood. The corporate executive who bought a Land Cruiser with all the added bells and whistles wanted people to see him as successful. The landscaper who bought the used Tundra wanted to tow his mower during the week and his boat on the weekends. The grandma who replaced her 25-year-old Camry with another Camry wanted familiarity and reliability. I sold these people attributes to make their lives go a little more smoothly.

The skills salespeople use to generate a high income are teachable. Even if you only try sales for a year or two, you will learn valuable skills that will help you succeed in any entrepreneurial endeavor. I was in sales throughout my 20s and didn't become a full-time entrepreneur until I was almost 30 years old. Without some level of sales ability, my first company would never have grown. I had to sell restaurant clients and recruit college kids to join my team, which would have been difficult without a sales background.

At the end of 2016, I had three modest income sources: Balloon Distractions, Life Leadership and royalties from my first book. I was driving an old Toyota Avalon with 188,000 miles on it when the car's air conditioning unit stopped working. It happened during first week in January, so I didn't worry much about it. I live in Tampa, and January is normally a mild month.

Just for kicks, I stopped at a Chevy dealership and took a new Chevy Volt out for a test drive. It was spiffy, quick off the line and high tech, but I didn't buy it. I refused to spend $30,000 for a depreciating asset.

A few days later, I found a used 2013 Volt selling for just over $14,000. I traded in my tired Avalon and bought my first plug-in vehicle. The Volt can drive for 35 miles on an electric charge before the gas generator starts powering the car.

A week later, I took my Volt on a 3,500-mile business trip through Atlanta, Louisville, Little Rock and Houston. Driving the Volt made me think about green tech and solar, so I began writing blog posts about these subjects.

Soon after that, I decided to get into the solar business. I didn't want to become an installer; that seemed too complicated, but I could bring my sales expertise to the industry. It would be easy to zip around Tampa in my Volt and just sell solar for another company.

For two weeks, I called several of the installers in my area, but none of them gave me the time of day. For some folks, this amount of discouragement would have been enough to make them quit, but I really wanted to find my way into the solar niche. I was determined.

I went to an Office Depot and bought a clipboard, then I printed a solar information sheet on my home computer and started knocking on doors. Within a few days, I had a decent stack of leads: homeowners who were interested in solar and wanted to get an estimate on their homes. I kept calling solar installers and finally met up with Steve Rutherford, the founder of Tampa Bay Solar. Steve wasn't sure if I was a good fit for his company. Other sales people had approached him in the past and had let him down. For the next few weeks, I knocked on doors and went with Steve on sales calls. I filled a notebook with notes while also learning about solar energy on the Internet. Within a couple of weeks, I was running sales calls and closing deals independently.

I didn't ask Steve to hire me as an employee, I merely asked for a percentage commission on all the deals that went through. This meant that I had the freedom to sell at my pace, on my schedule, on my terms.

This gave me the flexibility to allocate my time to my other income sources as needed. I found myself training a new balloon artist on some days, then changing my shirt to go out and sell a residential solar system.

I saw a huge opportunity in the emerging residential and commercial solar market. We are in the middle of a vast shift from the Industrial Revolution-fueled fossil fuels to the Conceptual Age powered by solar combined with electric vehicles.

Because of the sales ability that I've honed over the last 20 years, I was able to enter a brand new industry and earn an extra $5,000 (or higher) each month doing something totally new.

I found the right partner in Tampa Bay Solar; they have the install crew and the know-how to properly install whatever I sell. I'm also turning to Steve Rutherford as my mentor in that business.

I set up the expectations upfront; I wanted to have the freedom to sell on my own terms at a set commission. This means that I can still go fishing on Wednesday!

TRADITIONAL BUSINESS

If you have an original idea for a product or a service, you can always start small by simply going out into the world to try and sell it. Harland Sanders knew a market for his many herbs and spices existed because he had proved the concept. He had already increased the sales of the first KFC franchise in Salt Lake City. If Sanders's fried chicken recipe sold well in Utah, why couldn't it sell well elsewhere?

Someone's once-in-a-lifetime original idea can make that person a billionaire. In 1996, Sarah Blakely was a successful saleswoman in Orlando. Working in the Florida heat and humidity, she invented an undergarment similar to pantyhose that would allow her to wear open-toed shoes. It also made her figure look slimmer underneath her dress. Blakely called her invention Spanx.

Over the next year, Blakely patented her product and began pitching it to department stores. Neiman Marcus agreed to give Blakely a limited trial run in seven locations, so Blakely called all her friends and asked them to go into those locations to ask for Spanx by name.

At the same time, Blakely sent samples of Spanx to the Oprah Winfrey Show and landed on Oprah's coveted favorites list. That year, Spanx sold $4 million worth of products.

The company continued to grow from that point. Blakely landed a spot on QVC, selling thousands of pairs in just a few minutes. In 2015, Spanx generated $250 million in global sales, and Blakely is now worth over a billion dollars.

Sanders and Blakely weren't afraid to face rejection to sell a product. They started from scratch and put the right systems in place, creating a product that made sense and gained traction in the market.

Of course, it certainly helped that Sanders and Blakely created superior products. There was a lack of serious competition in their respective niches. Spanx was a better product than traditional pantyhose.

Pressure-cooked fried chicken tasted better than other chicken recipes. Not every idea has the billion-dollar potential of KFC or Spanx, but that doesn't mean those less profitable ideas aren't valuable. Just look at Steve Gadlin's cat artwork from his earlier chapter.

These are just some examples of the many types of traditional businesses people have started. When you launch a traditional business, you'll have to build business systems to help you run your company, sell your product and count your profits. A mentor who has already implemented these systems in a traditional business could help you in this area.

Going back to the last chapter, it makes sense to go out and learn how to sell your product or service before you hire employees, rent a warehouse or take on any other fixed business costs.

Jonathan Brewer with Earthworks built a prototype machine and went out on the road. He earned revenue using that early equipment. When I started Balloon Distractions in Tampa, I went out and sold restaurants on the idea first, even before I had a website or business cards. I ran that business out of my home; we made over $100,000 in total revenue in the first year. Most of that revenue was profit.

Traditional business is the toughest business model because you have no idea what will actually work in the open marketplace. Keep your operations small at first; build on reinvested profits rather than debt. If you can find a mentor, that's even better!

PATENTS AND LICENSING

In the 1930s and '40s, Disney licensed Mickey Mouse's image to certain manufacturers. Suddenly, the famous mouse was everywhere, and Disney didn't have to create any additional products. All of the companies that used the image paid a small royalty to Disney in exchange for the rights. The products with Mickey Mouse's image flew off the shelves, raking in revenue for both Disney and those licensed manufacturers.

Today, people see similar licensing arrangements for everything from movie characters to sports teams. These agreements can be hugely beneficial to a business's bottom line. For example, if a lunchbox company has a deal with Marvel that allows it to make lunchboxes emblazoned with the images of Iron Man or Captain America, that company will sell more units to young children than if the company sold only plain lunchboxes.

It's easy to see how licensing can benefit an established company creating a product that already has market value, but how does licensing benefit an unknown entrepreneur with an equally unknown product?

An entrepreneur must first prove that the product works in the marketplace before patenting an idea. Make some basic prototypes and try to sell the invention to the public. Get customer feedback; if no one wants the product, ask how the customers would improve on the item. Retain the contact information from those first customers and follow up later; if you give everyone a money back guarantee, you will gain a wealth of knowledge from customers who want a refund. Angry, yelling customers are nothing if not honest about how they feel.

With Balloon Distractions, I began checking all of my bookings via phone call. I used both the positive and negative data to improve my training program and make the system better. It's best to work out all the kinks in a product before patenting it. The idea may drastically change after the feedback period.

If an aspiring entrepreneur comes up with an idea for a product, that person might license the product to an established manufacturer. Always protect original ideas via patent before taking these ideas to larger companies.

There are many excellent resources out there for those wanting to patent a new invention. One book I recommend is *Patents, Copyrights & Trademarks for Dummies*. The patent process is expensive, so it makes sense to invest in some basic knowledge before hiring lawyers and paying consultants.

Once a patent is in place and there is an established demand for the patented invention, start calling manufacturers who already have products in that niche. If the idea is for a toy, you can pitch Mattel or Hasbro. If someone invents a better power tool, that person can talk to global brands like Craftsman. It will take persistence and some travel, but most large manufacturers will give a few minutes to look over a product. The important part is to get an appointment with someone who can move an idea up the flagpole and get it in front of the decision makers in that company.

If you become nervous about pitching a product, I'd highly recommend reading the sales books listed in previous chapters. If an invention makes sense and sells in the marketplace, an entrepreneur will have a much better chance of finding a manufacturer interested in licensing it.

When someone licenses an invention to a larger company, the company will manufacturer the product in its factory, distribute it and get it on retail shelves. An entrepreneur might only get a fraction of each sale, but that person can successfully sell his or her product without hiring an employee, carrying inventory or having to manufacture the actual product. If an invention sells well, the inventor can retire to a private island in the Bahamas and just count the money as it comes in each month.

Licensing requires you to come up with an original idea and patent it, so you may have to invest a couple thousand dollars in this process. The risk here is that you might not find anyone willing to do a license deal, in which case you would have to take the more expensive route of manufacturing and selling the product solo.

Licensing can also be a lucrative way for two well-known brands to come together and create added revenue. Look at the billion-dollar profits created when LEGO put together licensing deals with names like Star Wars and Harry Potter. LEGO tapped into the global popularity of these major brands and became the most profitable toy company in the world.

BUYING A FRANCHISE

A quick Google search for franchise opportunities will show many of the profitable ideas that people systematized and sold as franchises. Someone can buy a franchise that cleans gutters, serves chicken wings, takes care of the elderly or fixes motorcycles; the list is endless. There is no shortage of franchise ideas out there.

A company that sells a franchise is known as the franchisor, and the person who purchases a franchise is known as a franchisee.

When you become a franchisee, you are buying four things:

1. Wider brand recognition. Generally speaking, the larger the franchise, the more recognition the business will receive. The most common global franchisor is 7-Eleven with over 55,000 locations, but other big franchisors include McDonald's, KinderCare and Jiffy Lube. A traditional business starts with zero brand awareness in the wider marketplace, and a traditional business owner has to educate the public on what the business offers. Well-established brands have a logo that the community already recognizes. It would be hard to find a human being anywhere who had never seen the Golden Arches and then felt the subconscious need to order fries.

2. Initial and ongoing training. When a franchisee invests in a McDonald's franchise, the corporation will send the new owner to Hamburger University, an 80-acre facility in Oakbrook, Illinois. Over 80,000 owners and managers have trained at Hamburger University since 1961. This type of training takes new owners who know nothing about the fast food business and teaches them how to use the established McDonald's systems to run a profitable location.

3. Interconnected business systems that make the idea work. Every successful franchisor already has systems in place for tracking product, marketing, managing employees and paying out payroll. These systems

utilize tried-and-true technology and make it easier and more efficient to operate the new franchise.

4. Proven profitability. A franchisee is buying into a concept that has already succeeded in the marketplace. That person doesn't need to come up with a new, creative idea to amass wealth. Franchise systems are cookie-cutter; all the new owner has to do is pay attention to the training and work hard to make the business a success.

Like any business, there are downsides to running a franchise. Even with brand recognition and strong business systems in place, there are still franchise owners who fail. Here are some of the reasons you might avoid franchise ownership:

1. Expenses. Franchise fees are hefty and typically cost a minimum of $10,000. If a new business needs a physical location, a franchisee also pays for the building. Once you launch a franchise, you'll also have to pay an ongoing fee each month to the franchisor. With some companies, this fee is a percentage of gross sales; other franchisors charge each franchisee a flat monthly fee. When someone buys a franchise, that person will have to sign documents promising that franchise fee to the franchisor for as long as that franchise stays in business.

2. Long hours. A franchisee has to work at least 50 to 60 hours per week to make it work. Franchises like Chick-fil-A even prohibit franchise owners from holding any outside employment once they buy a franchise. The entrepreneurs who become wealthy owning franchises normally develop multiple stores and then put a management team in place. Most beginning franchisees work in their first store and live on savings until that location gets off the ground.

Marcus Price, the founder of Goin' Postal, is an example of a franchisor. His opinions on what makes a good franchise owner are clear.

"The most successful franchise owners we've seen are the people who are humble and just follow the system we've designed for them. The worst franchisees are the arrogant idiots with an MBA who buy a franchise, have never run a business in their life and come into our system acting like they know everything."

REAL ESTATE

Barbara Corcoran made her millions by building a sales organization that sold real estate. Many others have built wealth by investing in real estate. This chapter will delve into the investment side of real estate and what you can expect when investing.

Plenty of wealthy people have made a fortune from real estate; President Donald Trump is worth $3.5 billion today largely because of the real estate industry. Many entrepreneurs like the idea of real estate because it allows them to build a handsome residual or pipeline income.

On the flip side, there are also many people who have wiped themselves out investing in properties with hidden problems or tenant issues. Real estate investment can be highly lucrative, but it takes a keen mind and some serious chutzpah to be successful in this risky business.

For a decade, I owned a little rental home that cost $500 per month. I rented it out at $800 per month for a $300 monthly profit. Most of that gain disappeared when the renters moved out and I had to replace the carpet, paint the walls and fix the place for new tenants. My renters often stayed in 12 to 24-month periods, so I spent a lot of time and money doing these repairs.

I did most of the maintenance work myself and sometimes dragged my family in to do the painting when a tenant left. Despite this, I would inevitably break even. Whenever a repair was needed on the house, it seemed that it always happened when I was 1,000 miles away. I did it small with low risk and generated little to no profits.

The good thing about my investment scenario is that I did not go bankrupt trying to make a billion dollars. I eventually offloaded the little house with nothing wasted except time.

If you want to become a real estate tycoon, the best way to get started is to find a successful local mentor who owns many profitable buildings. Offer to do some repair work in exchange for business insight. The idea of being a real estate investor who owns 300 rental units and drives a Mercedes Benz might sound appealing and easy to the untrained eye, but real estate success takes many years of blood, sweat and sawdust.

Some beginning investors will buy a two-unit property and live in one of the units. That person will then rent out the second unit and use that money to pay down the mortgage. This a great way to become a property investor without taking a huge risk; the owner just has to make sure that he or she can afford the entire mortgage if the second unit sits empty or the renter conveniently forgets to pay rent. When a rental unit is vacant, it produces zero revenue; this happens to all property investors from time to time.

There are some municipalities that require landlords to meet specific requirements when taking on a renter. A real estate mentor will be aware of these requirements, which is why a mentor is so important. There are plenty of educational programs you can purchase that will claim to make an investor rich, but these programs are vague and will not teach you about your local market. An honest mentor will help more than any other resource.

Like any business, there are details in real estate investing that the infomercials will not show. To build a large enterprise, you have to go big; in order to go big, you must be able to work with debt.

As a real estate investor, I owned one home with a mortgage balance of $45,000. If I owned ten similar homes, I'd be on the hook for $450,000. If I owned 100 homes, I'd be sitting on 4.5 million in debt. That's a scary number for the average person.

As of 2016, President Trump had $600 million dollars in real estate debt, but his assets had a market value in excess of $3.5 billion. $600 million worth of debt is no big deal if you're worth $3.5 billion.

In his career, President Trump's companies have also declared bankruptcy four times. He was a huge risk taker, but it eventually worked out for him. For every President Trump success story, there are 100 stories about amateurs who invested in real estate and failed miserably. Real estate investment can be a great way for some folks to make it big, but it is always best to go into investments with a clear understanding of the risks.

STRATEGIC PARTNERSHIPS

The original strategic partnership was Reese's Peanut Butter Cups. Peanut butter is decent on its own; so is milk chocolate, but when someone combines both, it's an industry favorite. This is what happens when strategic partnerships go well; two concepts or businesses join forces to create something mutually beneficial.

In 2014, Walmart approached Marcus Price about placing his Goin' Postal concept in several Walmart locations in Florida. Goin' Postal now has franchises in 12 Walmart locations. If the partnership is successful, Goin' Postal could go from 250 to 2,000 franchise stores, benefitting both companies.

Recently, Google entered into a strategic partnership with eyewear seller Luxottica. As Google moves into the wearable computing devices industry, it makes sense to partner with a global firm that understands eyewear and has a distribution network ready to sell millions of Google Glass units.

Spotify and Uber teamed up in 2015 so that Uber riders could listen to custom music playlists in any Uber vehicle. The technology needs tweaks, but this concept adds value to both services and gives them an edge over competition in their respective markets.

GoPro entered a strategic partnership with Red Bull in 2009. Now, people can go online and find hours of footage featuring extreme sports feats courtesy of this union. Red Bull sponsors these videos while GoPro records the footage on their proprietary cameras. The partnership with Red Bull helped GoPro capture 50 percent of the action camera market. It probably sold a couple extra million cases of Red Bull as well.

Look at any business and think about what other industry might benefit from that brand. Red Bull makes energy drinks, and people who do extreme sports sometimes drink energy drinks. These same people also use video equipment to record their adventures. It was a natural partnership.

If you own a business and have a creative idea for a partnership, it never hurts to reach out to the marketing department of the target company. That wacky idea might be the next Reese's concept.

DIRECT SALES

Direct sales, also known as network marketing, is another low risk path to entrepreneurship.

As of 2015, the World Federation of Direct Selling Associations reported that the cumulative global sales from all direct sales companies was $184 billion. Amway was the leader with $9.5 billion in global sales.

Starting a Direct Sales business gives the average person an inexpensive path to entrepreneurship. If you spend $100 to start a business in this category and never earn any profits, your losses will be minimal.

Direct sales will teach you how to generate passive income without going into debt. The downside is that you have to learn how to build a team, but team-building is a valuable skill that you'll need to master in any business.

I was a business owner with the Quixtar network marketing business in 1998. Plugging into the Quixtar training taught me a ton about sales, team-building and leadership.

When I started Balloon Distractions in 2003, I used some of the residual income concepts from Quixtar to build my talent agency. When Balloon Distractions went national, it was because of concepts I borrowed from Quixtar's business training. I'll always be grateful for what I learned from Quixtar even though I never gained significant income from that source.

Most Direct Sales concepts have built-in systems; this is a huge advantage over starting a business from scratch. You won't have to spend time and money creating systems.

Any business owner in Direct Sales should avoid trying to sell a product or service that he or she does not use. It's difficult to convince a prospective customer of the merits of a product when the seller can't or won't use it. For example, I love the Mary Kay concept and philosophy, but I don't wear makeup and would therefore be a less effective salesman in that business.

Some people criticize network marketing because they failed to grow a team while in those businesses. Like any business, direct marketing takes hard work and consistent effort to build a compensated community.

I can only speak to my own experience within the Life Direct Sales company. I started building my team at the end of 2014. I earned $2500 in my best month. It's not a huge income, but I can use that extra money to pay off my home.

The Life material teaches anyone how to better manage their finances and go debt free. I used Life training to pay off over $185,000 in debt from 2014 to 2017.

In Direct Sales, the only limit to your income is the number of people who join your community. There are critics who accuse network marketing companies of being pyramid schemes, illegal enterprises or scams. I can only point to the longevity and business volume of the largest companies in the compensated community niche. Avon, Mary Kay, Amway and Tupperware are all well-known direct sales companies that generate billions of dollars each year in sales and share that money with their business owners. If these companies were truly scamming people, everyone would most likely know by now because authorities would have gotten involved. These concepts work, but they only work for people who are willing to get involved and work hard.

These companies generated a tremendous amount in global sales last year. Even if the corporate offices kept, say, 70 percent of the revenue, that still means 55 billion dollars went to the business owners in the field.

There are some network marketing companies that had flawed compensation plans and went bankrupt, but the same thing can happen to restaurant chains, banks, insurance companies and car manufacturers. There are many people who opened traditional businesses, bought rental properties or obtained franchises and watched those businesses tank. These people don't blame the business model when this happens in the same way that people scapegoat direct sales.

Direct Sales represents a low risk path to entrepreneurship, but it will require the same level of hard work and dedication as any other business. Your team will not grow until you share your concept with many people over a long period of time. Most of the people you talk to won't join your business, and out of all people who join your team, most of those folks won't grow the business.

The flip side of this is that you can find leaders over time who will take the ball and run with it. The toughest part of Direct Sales is just sticking with it and continuing to share the business with new people until your leaders emerge.

KNOW YOUR NUMBERS

Aspiring entrepreneurs should answer these three questions:

1. How much net income (after taxes) is coming into my household every month?
2. How much does my household spend each month?
3. After expenses are paid, how much is left over each month?

If you can't answer these three questions right away, you should hold off on starting any type of business. Managing the expenses for a household is similar to managing the expenses in a business. Sit down with a calculator and pad of paper to write down your monthly expenses. This is especially important to do in the context of marriage; there should be no secrets or hidden expenses between spouses.

Write down everything. If there are any bills to pay on a yearly or quarterly basis, do the math and break the bill up into monthly increments. You might not know how much you're actually spending, but the best way to find out is to look at receipts and credit card statements. When I first started doing this, I was shocked to find out that I had been spending $600 per month eating out with friends and family. Cooking at home is more work, but it costs far less than eating out or buying takeout.

There is no way to assess your finances without measuring your output and input. Lots of people do this exercise only to find they are losing money each month.

If your income is negative each month, you need to take drastic action. Downgrade to a less expensive car, sell some junk from the garage, stop spending money on luxuries and look for ways to create extra side income. Cancel your monthly obligations like cable TV!

I cut up my credit cards and moved to a debit card that would withdraw money from my account on the same day I used it. I now only use debit or cash. I drive a used vehicle and keep it maintained. My current goal is to pay off my four-bedroom home before my 45th birthday.

It may seem irrelevant to focus on personal finances in a business book, but the way you run your household finances will reflect in the way you run your business. Good household finances often beget good business finances.

A business owner should ask these four questions about the business each month:

1. How much total revenue did the business bring in this month?
2. How much were the total expenses this month?
3. How much was the monthly net profit for the business?
4. How much in taxes does the business owe on the net profit?

When a business starts to grow, bankers might try to offer attractive lines of credit to expand the business. Ignore these and invest profits from the business back into the business; never fund expansions with loans from banks. Business owners will have to pay back those loans with interest at a fixed rate, and this can be difficult if monthly revenue dips for whatever reason.

Shedding that debt and cleaning up your finances will remove stress from your life and give you peace of mind. This, in turn, will allow you to run a more successful business.

If you have crazy debt, buy some of the used paperback books written by authors like Dave Ramsey, Orrin Woodward or Chris Brady.

COLD WATER

I live in a planned subdivision in Florida; one of the benefits of this is access to a large swimming pool that remains open throughout the year. Florida is pretty warm from April to November, but it can be a bit chilly during the winter months. The pool doesn't get a lot of use during that time.

A few years ago, I began swimming later and later in the season, hitting the pool even when it was 50 degrees outside.

Eventually, I found myself swimming regularly even on the coldest winter days. I discovered that a daily swim in chilly water was great for my aching back and it strengthened my immune system.

The most challenging part of swimming in the cold is when you first get in the water. The cold water is shocking at first, but once you start moving and swimming across the pool, it gets easier. Swimming in cold water also requires breath control; the natural instinct of the body is to gasp when you first go under. I had to learn to override that response by breathing normally in a calm pattern.

Swimming in cold water is similar to finding success in business. The initial plunge is normally the most difficult part.

Mental toughness will be a large part of your success.

Going out to sell something is as simple as meeting up with people and having a friendly conversation. Most people will say no, but some folks will say yes. Enough people will eventually say yes, and the businessperson will eventually get better at sales through practice.

As an entrepreneur, you will face more rejection than in a regular job, but most entrepreneurs will also have more opportunity than in a regular job.

Compare this activity to that of people 200 years ago. Your distant ancestors probably toiled on farms and in factories for 80 hours a week, earning barely enough to feed themselves. Factory workers would often lose limbs, get sick and die before the age of 50.

Going further back, there were hunter-gatherers roaming the wild and killing animals for food. They had none of the comforts people enjoy today and lived short, brutal lives. Sometimes you ate the bear, but sometimes the bear ate you!

The average person in America has a roof over their head, a smartphone in their hand and the ability to read these words and comprehend these concepts. Even if you are very poor, you can still seek out a mentor and ask how to build a business. You have the ability to read this book and learn from it; you can start your path to entrepreneurial success today.

Marcus Price is a great example of this; he came to America completely homeless with a parachute and some camping gear, yet he built a large, successful company. I started Balloon Distractions with a bundle of balloons and less than $5 in my pocket.

Everyone will struggle and fail sometimes, but those people who go out and fail often will find out how to get better as long as they keep going and allow themselves time to master the craft.

Compared to humanity's ancestors, people today have it easy. Instead of hunting a wild animal for food and risking death, people now merely pitch a new client and risk rejection. I've faced rejection many times: when I was a young man in the dating world, when I sold energy deregulation contracts, when I asked restaurants to do business with Balloon Distractions and when I went on *Shark Tank*.

My many rejections eventually led me to clients who said yes. Some folks stayed with my company for a short time, some for many years. Each yes, no matter how small, was a building block for my business that allowed me to control my time and destiny as an entrepreneur. The biggest risk is truly in doing nothing.

The key here is to be proactive and not wait, to jump in the water and enjoy the cold. After all, there is no glory in waiting on the sidelines while others swim.

ABOUT THE AUTHOR

Ben T. Alexander is a lifelong learner and entrepreneur who has spent over 30 years studying the ins and outs of economics and effective leadership. Alexander founded many successful, lucrative businesses in various fields ranging from solar technology to children's entertainment. His most well-known company, Balloon Distractions, has appeared on the hit television show *Shark Tank* and is one of the largest talent agencies of its kind in the United States.

Alexander has also sung the National Anthem at NFL games, installed water filters in Honduras and taught rollerblading in Taiwan. Today, he lives in Tampa, Florida with his two daughters.

If you like this book and want to read more about what it takes to get on ABC's *Shark Tank*, check out *We Twist For Tips* on Amazon.com.

For press inquiries and other questions, please contact Ben at BenToddAlexander@msn.com.

Preliminary edits for this book were completed by Inëz Czymbor.
Final edits were completed by Ben T. Alexander.

www.ingramcontent.com/pod-product-compliance
Lightning Source LLC
Chambersburg PA
CBHW020454220526
45464CB00002B/982